A large spicebush swallowtail caterpillar *(Papilio troilus)* defends itself with false eyes.

This green scarab beetle *(Heterorrhina elegans)* pollinates flowers, as do many insects throughout the world.

Ultimate
BUG-OPEDIA

SECOND EDITION

THE MOST COMPLETE BUG REFERENCE EVER

DARLYNE MURAWSKI
& NANCY HONOVICH

NATIONAL GEOGRAPHIC
WASHINGTON, D.C.

CONTENTS

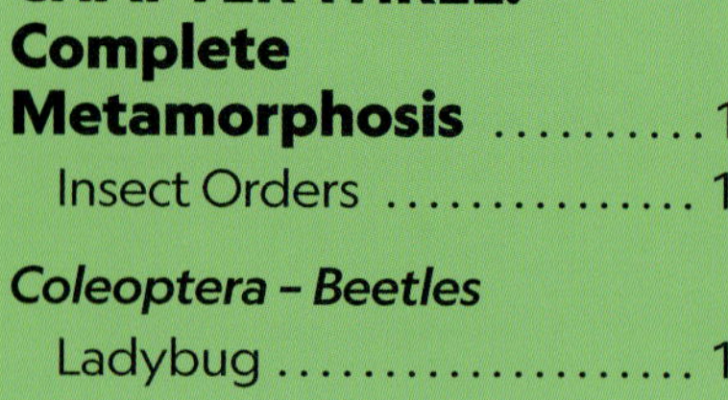

INTRODUCTION

Insects are endlessly fascinating. They come in many sizes, shapes, and colors. They walk, fly, jump, swim, and burrow. They eat many things—and many things eat them. As they grow, they often transform themselves from one shape into a very different one. A few are harmful to us, but overall we need insects for many reasons—and, in fact, we need them for our own survival.

As an entomologist, my job is to study insects. I find something surprising about every insect that I encounter.

The second edition of the *Ultimate Bugopedia* builds on the first book, showcasing more insects to better illustrate the incredible diversity of species on our planet. With more than 90 profiles of individual insects of different species and with many insect gallery spreads of even more insects within a group, along with hundreds of color photos throughout, this is a book that speaks to the life of insects. How do the bright colors of butterflies protect them from being eaten? Why do fireflies make their bodies flash? You'll find the answers to these questions and to just about anything else you want to know about insects in this book.

With *Ultimate Bugopedia* as your guide and inspiration, you can go to your backyard, or almost anywhere, to study insects on your own. Observe insects carefully, and you can make your very own scientific discoveries about them.

When I was young, no single book encompassed the diversity of insect life like this one does. So you are lucky. With *Ultimate Bugopedia* as your companion, I hope that you will discover the world of insects and become as fascinated with it as I am.

Bill Lamp, Ph.D.
entomologist and expert consultant
for *Ultimate Bugopedia*

Welcome to the *Ultimate Bugopedia*—a big source for information on the fascinating world of insects, with more than 450 photos. Insects are the most abundant and successful group of animals on Earth—with more than a million known species and many more yet to be discovered. As a scientist and as a writer, I enjoyed working on this book, and I hope you will enjoy reading it.

When I was a child, I loved observing "bugs" and exploring nature outdoors. Those times provided endless small discoveries for me—like how bees visited different flowers in our garden at different times of day and how butterflies would try to stick their proboscises in the center of each flower on my brightly colored shirt!

My early enthusiasm for insects started me on a path toward pursuing my interests in a big way. As an adult, I've been fortunate to work as a biologist who studies butterflies and plants, and as a nature photographer who photographs them. In my travels around the world to places like Thailand, India, and the Amazon region of South America, I've encountered countless insects with amazing adaptations for survival. You can see some of my photos of them in this book.

You may find yourself with a similar fascination for insects and their relatives. Some of the insects profiled in this book will be familiar to you, and others won't. The insects you'll see are from various parts of the world, and each has a story to tell. Enjoy exploring *Ultimate Bugopedia*. You'll find another great thing about insects: You can never outgrow your interest in them. I haven't.

Darlyne Murawski, Ph.D.
biologist, nature photographer,
and author of *Ultimate Bugopedia*

HOW TO USE THIS BOOK

***U**ltimate Bugopedia* is filled with information about insects and a few of their relatives, including spiders. Here you will find a guide to some of the pages in the different chapters.

The first chapter, "Discovering Bugs," is an introduction to everything about these amazing animals. It will help you learn about and understand them, so that when you read the profiles of individual species, you'll already be in the know. The "Life Cycle of an Insect" is one topic explored in this section.

The second and third chapters, the largest parts of the book, feature profiles of different insect species. They are organized by the type of metamorphosis that the insects undergo: simple or complete. The insects are then further arranged by their groups or orders. The pages at the right show insect orders for complete metamorphosis.

There are 92 individual profiles of insect species in the book. Here is an example of one of them.

PAPER WASP
FAMILY VESPIDAE

Paper wasps are the builders of the insect world, with a real knack for nest construction. To build their nests, most paper wasp species begin by gathering fibers from dead wood and plants. They mix the materials together with their saliva, then shape the mixture into clusters of comb-shaped cells. When the nest cells dry, they have a paperlike quality. The nests are also water-repellent, which keeps them dry in the rain. The wasps build their nests in sheltered areas, including tree branches and the eaves of houses. For added protection, the wasps secrete a chemical around their nest. The chemical repels ants that would otherwise feed on the eggs stored inside the nest.

FACTS

OTHER COMMON NAME	Umbrella wasp
SCIENTIFIC NAME	Subfamily: Polistinae / Family: Vespidae
SIZE	Under 0.7–1 inch (18–25 mm)
WINGS	Yes
FOOD	Adult: nectar and honeydew / Larva: insects such as caterpillars
HABITAT	Urban areas, meadows, and grasslands
RANGE	Worldwide

Scientists have discovered that ONE PAPER WASP SPECIES, Polistes fuscatus, CAN RECOGNIZE INDIVIDUALS OF ITS TYPE BY THE PATTERNS ON THEIR FACES. Their ability to recognize faces is much like our own ability to do so!

This paper wasp works on building the cells of its nest. Some paper wasp nests contain 200 cells.

190

BUTTERFLIES GALLERY

Butterflies have amazing wings made up of thousands of tiny scales. These scales can be brightly colored or dull, and even transparent. Some butterflies have shiny, metallic colors, like the morpho.

Butterflies use their wing colors and patterns in many ways. They can be used for camouflage, to absorb heat, and to find a mate. Some toxic butterflies also rely on their bright colors to warn predators that they taste foul. Potential enemies, like birds, learn to keep away. With about 20,000 butterfly species, these fluttering insects live just about anywhere in the world. They can be found in rainforests, mountaintops, deserts, cities, and even your own backyard. Do you have a favorite of the species shown here?

The peacock butterfly lives in Europe and parts of Asia. Its flashy eye-spots may help deter predation. Adult butterflies hibernate over the winter.

A Malayan zebra butterfly drinks from moist, rocky soil. In Southeast Asia, these butterflies are often seen mud-puddling with other butterflies.

A small skipper butterfly rests at attention on a flower stalk. Skippers have strong wing muscles for darting in flight.

A close-up of a butterfly's iridescent wing scales. The optically formed colors that you see depend on the angle at which you look at the wings.

The Cairns birdwing is Australia's largest native butterfly. It inhabits the rainforests of Queensland on the northeast coast.

This cattleheart butterfly is a type of swallowtail butterfly. Its fuzzy thorax is covered in tightly packed black and red hairs.

252

253

Throughout the book, there are photo galleries—13 in all—that will show you even more species within a group than the ones individually profiled. The butterflies gallery above is one example.

BANDED DEMOISELLE

A SCORPIONFLY ON A LEAF

LADYBUGS (LADYBIRD BEETLES) ON A VINE TENDRIL

STINK BUG NYMPHS JUST AFTER HATCHING FROM THEIR EGGS

TREE NYMPH BUTTERFLY

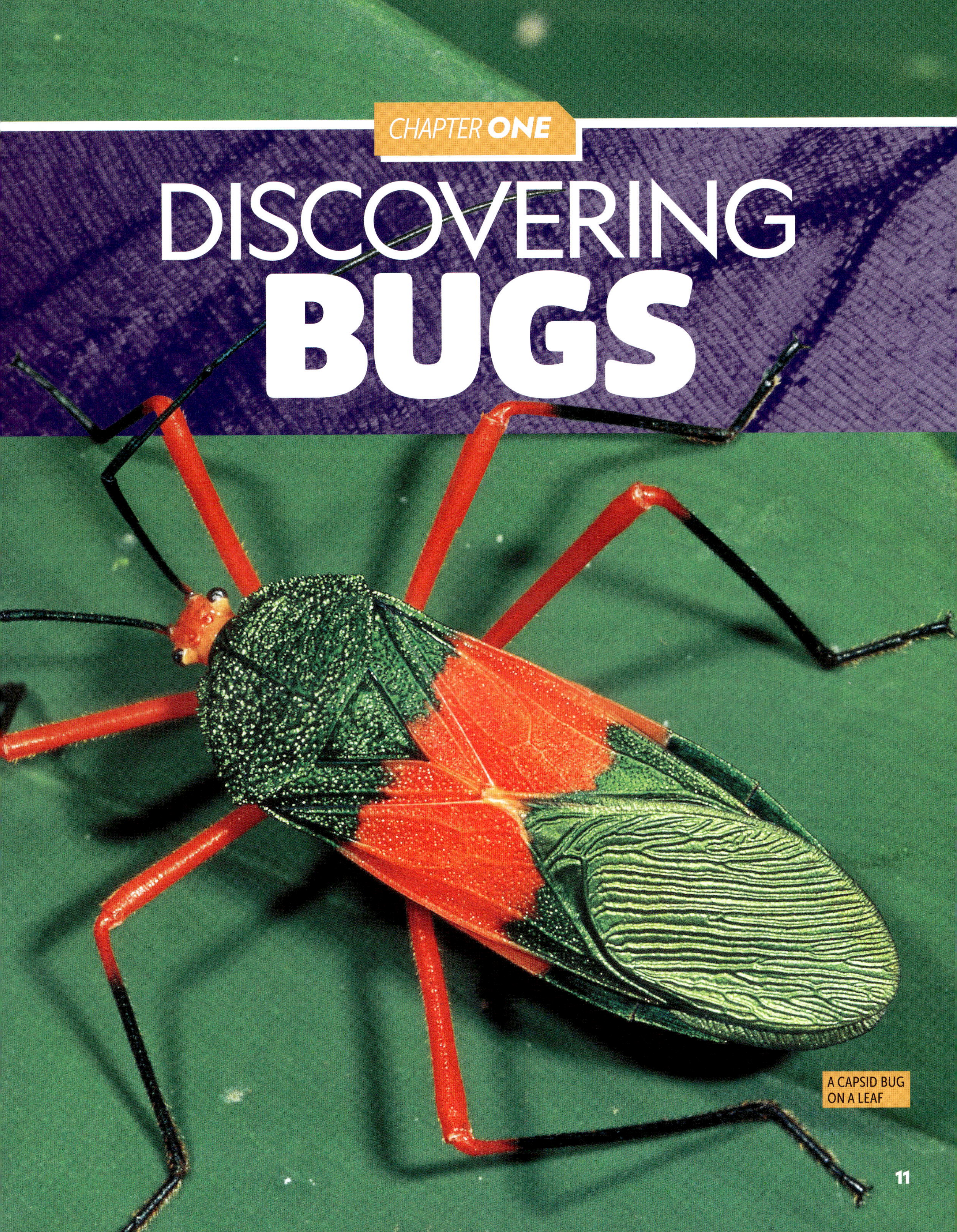

DISCOVERING BUGS

WHAT IS A BUG?

Look around you. It's not hard to find bugs. They crop up just about anywhere. But let's start off by thinking about what a bug actually is. To many, a bug is any small critter that looks vaguely like an insect, spider, or worm. To an entomologist, a scientist who studies insects, a bug refers to a specific group of insects called "true bugs." But generally, and in this book, the word "bug" is used to mean "insect." Not all of what we sometimes think of as bugs are insects, though: spiders and worms, for instance, aren't insects.

Insects have a hard external skeleton, called an exoskeleton. They have no spine, like we have. Along with other spineless animals, they are called invertebrates. Invertebrates also include spiders, worms, jellyfish, sponges, snails, crabs, and octopuses. Of all the invertebrates, insects are the only ones that evolved wings.

All insects have certain features in common. They have three main body sections: the head, the thorax, and the abdomen. On their heads, most insects have eyes and two antennae.

This cicada has two large compound eyes and three small, pink simple eyes.

SCIENTIFIC CLASSIFICATION OF THE DRAGONFLY

Scientists divide animals into groups to help our understanding. Here's how the dragonfly gets grouped.

Kingdom:	Animalia (animals)
Phylum:	Arthropoda (jointed legs; or more precisely, "jointed foot")
Class:	Insecta (insects)
Order:	Odonata (dragonflies and damselflies)
Family:	Libellulidae
Genus:	*Trithemis*
Species:	*Trithemis pallidinervis* (long-legged marsh glider)

The eyes can be compound or simple. Most insects have both types of eyes, but some only have one or the other. On its thorax, an adult insect has six legs. Beyond these common features, insects have differences, such as types of mouthparts, wings, and shape of antennae, that separate them into various groups.

Insects breathe through pores in their bodies called spiracles. (See the blue circles on the caterpillar above.) The spiracles lead to tubes called tracheae inside the body. Insects don't have lungs, but like other animals, they breathe by taking in oxygen and letting out carbon dioxide. In some cases, their muscles expand and contract to control the intake of air.

INSECTS' CLOSEST RELATIVES

Insects are members of a larger group of animals we call arthropods. Their closest relatives are members of this group. Besides insects, other arthropods include arachnids (spiders, mites, and scorpions), crustaceans (crabs, lobsters, shrimp, and barnacles), myriapods (millipedes and centipedes), sea spiders, and horseshoe crabs. Of all the arthropods on Earth, insects make up the vast majority of species.

Arthropods have jointed legs. They also have a segmented body and a hard external skeleton, or exoskeleton. The inside of an arthropod is a cavity full of fluids. These internal fluids are similar to our blood.

This scorpion has powerful claws for grasping and a venomous stinger on the tip of its long, segmented abdomen.

A red ghost crab from Chandipur, India. Its head and thorax are fused together and covered by a hard shell called a carapace. The crab's eyes are on stalks that help it see in all directions.

An argiope spider in its web. Spiders—along with scorpions, ticks, and mites—differ from insects in the number of body parts and legs they have.

Horseshoe crabs from Thailand. These arthropods are not true crabs but are related to extinct sea scorpions. The hinged shell covers the crab's body, including its legs.

FOSSIL BUGS

Throughout their history, when insects died, some of them left behind impressions or imprints of themselves, which became fossilized.

According to these fossil records, the first winged insects were mayflies, grasshoppers, and cockroaches. They appeared about 350 million years ago. That's about 120 million years before the appearance of the earliest dinosaurs!

Then, over a period of time that began 145 million years ago, the first flowering plants appeared. As flowering plants evolved, an explosion of diverse forms of insects followed—many of which were pollinators (like bees) and plant-eaters (like butterfly and moth larvae).

Ancient insects became fossilized if they met certain conditions. Some fell into sticky tree resin that over the years turned into a transparent, golden, stonelike substance called amber. Insects that were fossilized in amber reveal lots of detail. Other insects were buried in materials like clay and sand that over millions of years turned into sedimentary rock. Inside the rock, the insect's flattened body made an imprint (or impression). Certain fossils can reveal more than just an impression. They can also hold the blackened (carbonized) remains of the insect. Other fossils are mineralized replacements of the original insect, meaning that the space that once held the insect's body was filled in over time with minerals.

WHERE INSECTS GO IN WINTER

Depending on the species, they may migrate to warmer locations, find shelter from the cold, or hibernate until warmer weather. Many insects have a type of antifreeze in their body that keeps ice crystals from forming. They may hibernate at any point in their life cycle.

A beetle fossilized in Baltic amber from about 50 million years ago

A prehistoric grasshopper preserved in amber

This is the oldest known full-bodied fossil of a flying ancient insect, which resembles a dragonfly. It is estimated to be 312 million years old and was found in Massachusetts, U.S.A. When the insect was alive, it left its imprint in mud.

INSECT DIVERSITY

About one million species of insects have been described and named. Sometimes it takes years after discovery to describe and name a new species. It's hard to say exactly how many insects there are worldwide because new species are being described all the time, so the number is always increasing. But that's not all. There are many more species that have yet to be discovered.

Scientists have only been able to come up with rough estimates of the total number of insect species in the world. And those estimates range from three million to upwards of 30 million species, with some experts agreeing on an estimate of around 10 to 30 million. This means there are plenty of new insects for future generations of scientists—like you—to discover and study!

Insects and other invertebrates make up 96 percent of all animal species. Only about 4 percent of animal species are vertebrates, the animals people are most familiar with (including mammals, birds, reptiles, amphibians, and fish).

Insect diversity is highest in the tropical areas of the world, especially in the treetops of the rainforest. In tropical rainforests, a large portion of the insects are beetles and small wasps. In the coldest climates, insect diversity is the lowest. Some insect groups found in the coldest climates include icebugs, dagger flies, and balloon flies.

Some insects are found over a large area that covers different continents, while others have smaller distributions. Often, nonmigratory insects that live in isolated places like on islands and mountaintops are not found anywhere else.

This snail is but one of many invertebrates.

Mammals, like this tiger, make up less than one percent of all animals.

DIVERSITY OF THE ANIMAL KINGDOM

INVERTEBRATES **95.6%**

MAMMALS **0.4%**

AMPHIBIANS **0.5%**

REPTILES **0.6%**

BIRDS **0.7%**

FISH **2.2%**

PERCENTAGE OF INVERTEBRATES BY GROUP

INSECTS **71.1%**

MOLLUSKS **8.5%**

CRUSTACEANS **4.3%**

SPIDERS **3.1%**

OTHER INVERTEBRATES **13.0%**

LIFE CYCLE OF AN INSECT

After hatching from its egg, a young insect grows until its skin, or exoskeleton, gets too tight. Then it must shed its old skin, or molt. As it grows, an insect goes through a series of stages between molts.

Insects also go through some developmental changes as they mature. These changes are referred to as metamorphosis. There are two kinds of metamorphosis: simple and complete.

In species such as grasshoppers and true bugs, which undergo **simple metamorphosis,** there are three stages: the egg, nymph, and adult. The immature insect is called a nymph. Nymphs generally look like miniature versions of the adult, minus the wings. In species that develop wings, the nymphs have little wing buds visible on their backs.

In species such as butterflies, moths, and beetles, which go through **complete metamorphosis,** there are four stages: the egg, larva, pupa, and adult. The juvenile insect is called a larva. The larva looks very different from the adult insect. In order to transform into an adult, it must first go through an inactive stage, when it is called a pupa. During this stage, the larval tissues break down and adult tissues form—including the wings. When the time is right, a newly formed adult breaks out of the pupal skin and expands its wings. For protection, some insect larvae spin a silk cocoon before transforming into a pupa. The cocoon is a protective covering, like a blanket.

LIFE CYCLE OF A GRASSHOPPER:
SIMPLE METAMORPHOSIS

The two-striped grasshopper *(Melanoplus bivittatus)* typically lays its eggs in soil, where they will stay over winter. In the spring, when they hatch, tiny nymphs emerge and begin eating plants. As the nymphs grow, they molt a few times. At each stage of their development, their future wings grow. When the nymph molts for the last time, the emerging adult has fully developed wings and can fly.

LIFE CYCLE OF A MONARCH BUTTERFLY:
COMPLETE METAMORPHOSIS

1. EGG

After an egg is laid, a caterpillar develops inside. Upon hatching, the caterpillar begins feeding and growing. It molts a few times whenever its body gets too large for its exoskeleton.

4. ADULT

Eventually, the exoskeleton of the pupa cracks open and the adult butterfly slides out. It hangs onto its old exoskeleton until its wings have hardened and it is ready to fly.

3. PUPA

2. LARVA

The caterpillar turns into a pupa. At first the pupa is green. But as the adult butterfly forms inside, its black, orange, and white colors become visible.

1. EGGS

2. NYMPH

3. ADULT

COURTSHIP, MATING, AND EGG-LAYING

Finding a suitable mate is a challenge for insects. In addition to visual cues like color patterns, airborne chemicals called pheromones help insects locate possible mates. Courtship can involve dancing, gift giving, serenading, touching, and blinking their lights to entice a partner to mate. Many insects also use sound or surface vibrations.

The mating process involves contact between a male and female in order to fertilize the eggs. Hoverflies, butterflies, and other winged insects sometimes even mate in flight.

After laying eggs, most insects don't hang around to care for their young. That doesn't mean they don't try to improve their offspring's chances of survival, though. Insects may prepare nests in advance or carefully select just the right host plant for laying their eggs.

Species in which one or both of the parents care for their young include social insects like ants, wasps, and termites. (See "Social Insects" on pages 40–41.)

The male dance fly courts the female by offering her a nuptial gift. She eats the gift while mating.

After courtship, a pair of tiny hairstreak butterflies mate on a leaf, after which the female will seek host plants where she can lay her fertilized eggs.

To find a mate, a male *Creatonotos gangis* moth turns its greenish scent organ inside out from the end of its abdomen. It secretes a pheromone that attracts females of its species.

A stink bug in the process of laying her eggs

INSECT EGGS AND EGG CASES

Female insects tend to lay many eggs—up to thousands over their lifetime. By laying so many eggs, they improve the chances that a few of their young will survive. Insect eggs come in many different shapes, colors, and sizes, depending on the species. The eggs might be bundled in silk cases, or set in jellylike (gelatinous) masses. Some eggs have long stalks, and some are glued to tree branches. The females of most types of insects lay eggs, but aphids, some moths and flies, and a few cockroach species give birth to live young, meaning the eggs hatch before the babies are born.

A leopard lacewing butterfly laying her eggs on a leaf

A large cluster of cabbage butterfly eggs

A cockroach laying an egg case full of eggs

Many young mantises stream out of the bottom of an egg case made by their mother.

Some lacewings lay their eggs on the end of a stalk, which may then attach to a plant, wood, or even a windowsill.

PUPAE

The pupa is the resting stage between larva and adult in insects that undergo complete metamorphosis. Pupae may appear quiet on the outside, but on the inside, their larval body is breaking down and their new body as a winged adult is forming. The seemingly helpless pupae have some special ways of protecting themselves. A few are able to wriggle or even walk around if touched. Some pupae can make sounds or vibrate to scare predators. Some secrete toxic chemicals to avoid being eaten. Others, especially certain butterfly pupae, are defended by ants. (See the alcon blue butterfly on page 242.) The pupae of bees, wasps, and ants remain in their hives or nests and are protected by adults of their species. Other insects spend their time as pupae underground, on trees and branches, or underwater.

A black swallowtail caterpillar transforming into a pupa. It is supported by a silk strand connecting it to the branch.

A mosquito pupa floating near the surface of the water. It leaves the water as an adult.

A monarch butterfly emerges from its pupal exoskeleton. Once out, the butterfly will hang from the exoskeleton as its wings expand.

A tomato hornworm caterpillar under attack by parasitoid wasps. After feeding on the caterpillar, the wasp larvae spin white silk cocoons and turn into pupae inside it.

An adult worker ant carrying a pupa

BUG SENSES

GULF FRITILLARY BUTTERFLY

Bugs have the same senses of sight, taste, smell, hearing, and touch that we do, but their senses work in very different ways from our own. Imagine if we could taste with our feet and hear with ears on our legs, or see in front of and behind us at the same time.

TASTE

Insects taste mainly with their mouthparts and their feet. Some insects, such as bees, also have taste receptors on their antennae. And female wasps and crickets can determine by taste where to lay their eggs, using the egg-laying organ (ovipositor) on the end of their abdomen.

TOUCH

An insect's sense of touch comes from the small hairs on its body that have a nerve at their base. Insects can feel if these hairs touch another object or if there are changes in air movement around them.

SIGHT

Insects see with simple or compound eyes—many have both types, and a few have no eyes at all. Simple eyes can't focus on images, but merely distinguish between light and dark. Many larvae and termites have simple eyes. Compound eyes, with their faceted lenses, can see objects in color and detail. Insects with large compound eyes can see in all directions. A honeybee's compound eyes are able to see a wider range of colors than most insects because they have three color pigment receptors, like us, rather than the two that most insects have.

SMELL

The antennae act as an insect's nose. They are covered in smell-gathering receptors that make them sensitive to odor molecules in the air. Besides being used for smell, antennae put insects in touch with the environment in other ways. For example, antennae can also detect humidity. Mosquitoes use their antennae to detect sound, and to assess air speed as they fly.

HEARING

Many insects don't have the ability to hear. Of those that do, their ears can be on various parts of the body—usually the thorax or abdomen, but sometimes on their front legs. Crickets, grasshoppers, katydids, and cicadas are among the insects that can hear. Certain moths have ears. Hearing allows these moths time to drop to the ground and play dead when bats approach them at night.

ANTENNAE

Insect antennae come in many forms. The antennae are made up of a row of segments. Each segment is jointed, so the antennae bend, and each segment can have its own shape. The segments can be simple and straight—like those of mayflies, cockroaches, and caddisflies. The antennae can be clubbed on the ends, as in butterflies. They can be rounded or platelike, as in many beetles. And they can be feathery, like those of many moths and flies. In ants and weevils, the antennae are bent in the middle.

A red admiral butterfly. Butterfly antennae are knobbed on the tips. They can detect the smells of nectar and pheromones.

The male cecropia moth has large feathery antennae. It is in the same silk moth family as the luna moth on page 29. Females have thinner antennae than males.

Male mosquitoes, like this one, have very thick, feathery antennae. They use them to find females of their species. In contrast, females have thinner feathery antennae.

Male ten-lined June beetles have huge antler-like antennae that help them locate females.

This Asian longhorn beetle has very long antennae typical of its family, Cerambycidae.

Only the male glowworm beetle has ornate, comb-like antennae. The females are larger than the males and look like larvae.

A capsid bug using a pair of its legs to clean its left antenna. Insects typically spend a lot of time grooming to stay clean and keep their senses sharp.

HOW BUGS "TALK"

People communicate both verbally and nonverbally with other people. We talk, make noises, make faces, gesture, touch, and use scents.

Insects do similar things. They communicate with sounds, visual signals, touching, and also by using their sense of smell. They communicate in order to find mates, escape predators, mimic other insects, warn of danger, threaten others, and give directions to food sources or other resources.

Insects make sounds by rubbing their body parts together (called stridulating), and by hissing, tapping, and vibrating their wings or special sound-producing membranes. They communicate visually with color patterns, body movement, and light flashes. Several types of insects, such as fireflies and glowworms, have light-emitting organs that glow in the dark.

Touching is an especially important form of communication for insects that can't hear and don't see well. For example, when ants and termites run in a line, they use their antennae to tap the hind legs of the individual in front of them, as if to say "I'm still behind you."

Insects communicate by smell using chemical odors called pheromones. They emit these odors, or messages, into the air. In addition to the pheromones that attract mates, insects use other odors in making food trails and for sounding the alarm to members of their species when danger is near.

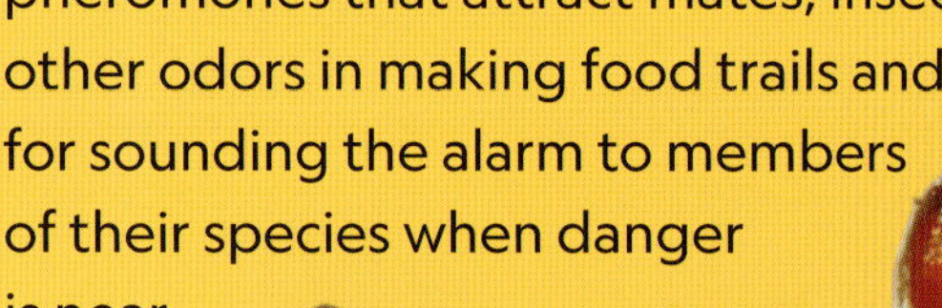

This pyralid moth communicates its desire to mate by wafting pheromones in the air. It does this by extending "hair pencils" from its abdomen and waving its abdomen from side to side.

Fireflies "talk" to each other with light signals (below). The pattern of blinking can signal different things, such as an interest in finding a mate or in defending a territory.

Ants communicate with each other through visual signals, sounds, touch, and pheromones. The two ants at left, with their powerful jaws, are threatening to attack each other.

FOOD AND FEEDING

Many insects—especially those with complete metamorphosis—change what they eat when they grow up. For example, the caterpillars of butterflies and moths typically chew leaves, but as adults they drink nectar or other liquids.

An insect's mouthparts correspond with its diet. For instance, the proboscis of many butterflies and moths is long and hollow for reaching into flowers to drink nectar. The proboscis coils up when the meal is over. The group of insects called true bugs have a combined proboscis and hardened beak to pierce plants and drink their sap. Both mosquitoes and aphids can pierce and suck—the mosquito to feed on animal blood and the aphid to feed on plant fluids. Insects that chew their food feed with a pair of mandibles that can cut, tear, and crush. Meat-eating insects tend to have knifelike mandibles, whereas plant-eating insects have flatter, wider ones. Some mandibles are modified for fighting and hunting.

Host plants are the source of food for many larval and adult insects. Some insects can survive on only one species of host plant. For this reason, these species are called specialists. Other insects can eat various plants and are considered generalists. The larvae of a few generalists, like the spongy moth, will eat just about any kind of leaf. Large groups of them can remove the leaves from a patch of forest.

A praying mantis holds a grasshopper with a viselike grip while feeding on it.

10 COOL BUG MOUTHS

WHERE BUGS LIVE

Insects are found just about anywhere on Earth—from the polar regions to rainforests, from treetops to underground, as well as underwater, in houses, on animals, and on and inside of plants. One group of insects called sea skaters is even found on the surface of the ocean. Over time, insects have adapted to every available habitat where they can find resources. Special adaptations allow them to survive in places with extreme conditions, such as the freezing-cold Arctic, and the dry Namib desert, which in some areas gets less than a half inch (13 mm) of rain per year. With the exception of a few species of water strider, there are no insects in the open ocean.

Many insects require more than one habitat over their life spans. For example, some insects may live underground or underwater as larvae or nymphs, and aboveground as adults.

These termites march with nest-mates in search of new sources of dead wood in the forest.

Mosquitoes are found in moist environments, and their larvae live in standing water. Adult females need occasional blood meals.

Flies are attracted to warm and moist places like animal dung (feces), where they lay their eggs.

A spotted cucumber beetle on a flower. It sometimes feeds on pollen when it's not eating the green parts of plants.

Leaf miners are the larvae of several types of insects that feed on an inner layer of leaf tissue, making visible trails as they move along.

Wasps often build their nests in protected locations, like under the eaves of houses.

Caterpillars can often be found on the under-surface of leaves, where they're less visible to passing birds.

Whirligig beetles twirl around on the surface of flowing streams. They can swim, dive, and fly.

INSECTS IN NATURE

Insects form an important link in the food chain. They provide food for birds, lizards, mammals, fish, amphibians, spiders, and other insects. If insects were to disappear off the face of the Earth, there would be a chain reaction, and many other animals and plants that depend on them would become extinct. We rely on insects to pollinate crops, make honey, make silk, and clean up the environment. Scientists use insects like *Drosophila* flies (fruit flies) for research. Gardeners use predatory insects to get rid of plant-eating pests. And in some parts of the world, people eat protein-rich insects as part of their diet.

Small as they are, insects play major roles in the environment, and whether they are herbivores, predators, parasites, or parasitoids determines what part they play. They are herbivores if they feed on plants; predators if they kill small animals for food; parasites

Parasites feed on many insects. Some are fairly harmless, like the tiny mites covering this beetle.

A green anole lizard with a fly in its mouth

if they get their nutrients from living on or inside another animal without killing it; and parasitoids if they live as parasites but eventually kill their host.

Insects may engage in a "mutualistic" partnership with other organisms such as plants. This means that both the plant and the insect benefit from each other. A classic example of mutualism is pollination. The plant gets fertilized, and the insect typically gets rewarded with nectar, pollen, or resin. About 80 percent of flowering plants depend on insects for pollination—and that includes many of our crop plants, such as apples and broccoli.

Some insects have a special role in cleaning up the environment. They may chew up the wood of fallen trees, recycle animal dung, and even break down dead animal bodies. They perform tasks that people don't want to do, and by burrowing and burying, they do wonders to improve the soil.

A bumblebee drinks nectar and gets covered in pollen.

After attacking a beetle, these ants will carry it back to their nest.

SOCIAL INSECTS

Some insects are solitary and others naturally group together, like a cluster of ladybugs or certain caterpillars, when they feed in a row on the edge of a leaf. But truly social (or eusocial) insects have a system with special tasks for each member. Social insects include all ants, all termites, and many bees and wasps.

Social insects have certain features in common. They live together in a nest. They tend their young. They have overlapping generations—meaning that new insects are constantly being produced in a colony—and they have a division of labor, or caste system, in which members carry out specific tasks. Their castes include "reproductives," which are the queens and drones. The task of queens and drones, besides reproducing, is to select a location for a colony and to begin preparing the new nest. Other caste members, including workers and soldiers, don't reproduce. Workers are responsible for cleaning the nest; caring for eggs, larvae, pupae, and the queen; and collecting food. Soldiers defend the colony from predators.

The nymphs of true bugs often group together as a large family. They are social in one sense, but not eusocial like insects with a caste system.

Worker ants from one colony of weaver ants are working together to bridge a gap between two leaves. Once the bridge is established, other ants can cross over it.

Workers of a paper wasp colony build the hive and tend the young. If the queen wasp happens to die, one of the workers will replace her.

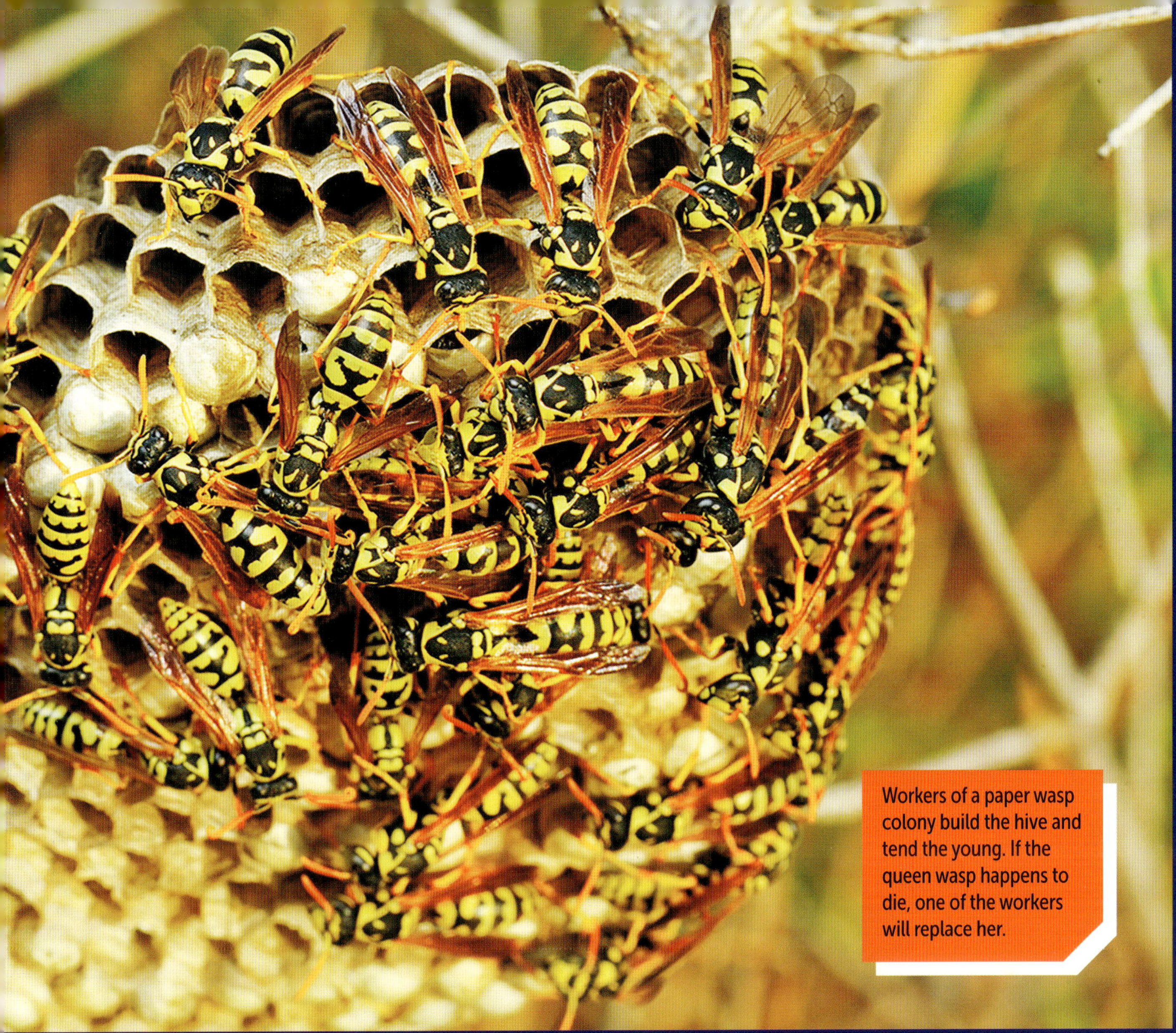

SIZE DIFFERENCE IN **LEAFCUTTER ANTS**

Look at the difference in shape and relative size of these three leafcutter ants. They belong to the same species—*Atta cephalotes*. The largest is a queen, whose sole responsibility is to reproduce, and the other two are workers: a major and a minor.

1. QUEEN

2. MAJOR

3. MINOR

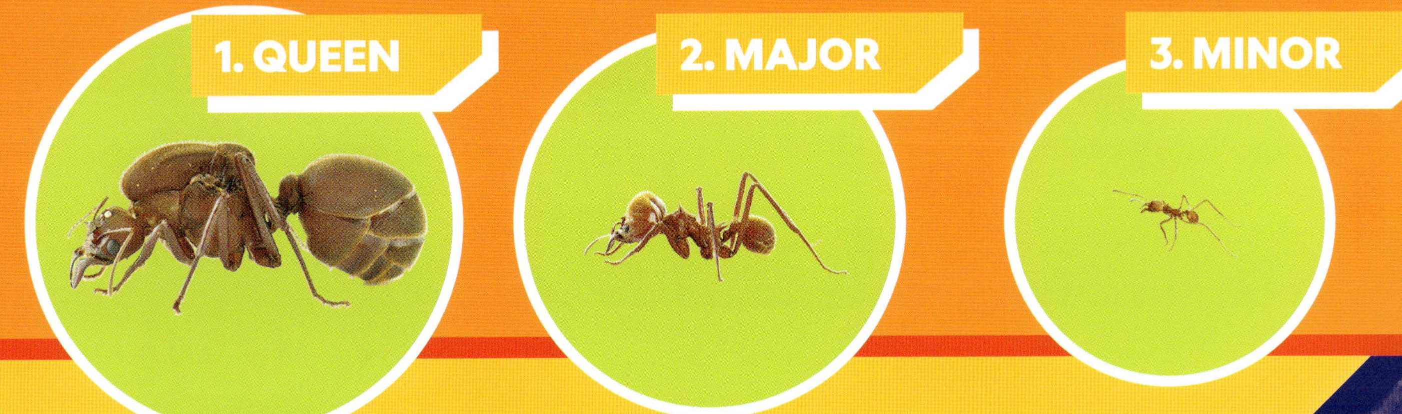

COLORS AND PATTERNS

The incredible colors and designs on insects like beetles and butterflies help them to recognize each other, to impress mates, and to avoid predators. The colors and patterns are mostly determined by an insect's genes.

The colors seen in insects are produced in two different ways. One is by chemical pigments (or dyes) in their outer bodies and wing scales. The other is by the reflection of light off the three-dimensional texture on the surface of the insects' bodies. This is called structural coloration. Insects with structural coloration can look metallic or iridescent—shifting as you see them from different angles.

The scales covering the wings and bodies of butterflies and moths can have either type of color and often have both. The striking, iridescent wings of blue morpho butterflies and Madagascan sunset moths are examples of structural colors. Flies, dragonflies, and other clear-winged insects have structural color patterns that they display by holding their wings at certain angles.

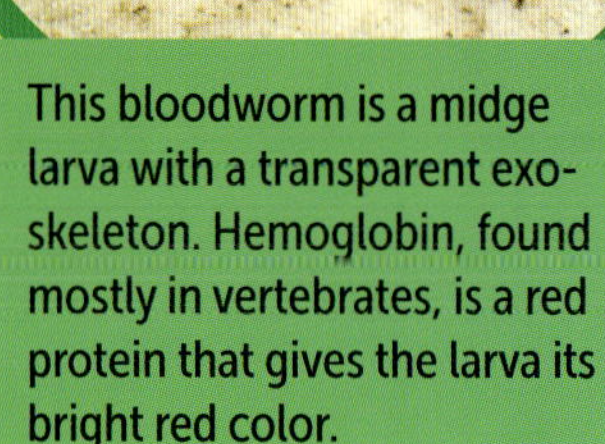

This bloodworm is a midge larva with a transparent exo-skeleton. Hemoglobin, found mostly in vertebrates, is a red protein that gives the larva its bright red color.

The Madagascan sunset moth has iridescent green on the forewings and various iridescent colors on the hind wings.

A rose chafer beetle on a rose leaf. Its green metallic-looking body can shift colors as it moves around.

Close-up of iridescent blue scales from a butterfly's wing. The fine texture on each scale produces the color we see.

An iridescent blue-green damselfly with dark-colored wings

DEFENSES

Being near the bottom of the food chain, insects are surrounded by predators—mammals, birds, reptiles, amphibians, fish, and various arthropods. As a result, they have evolved an incredible array of defenses in order to survive. Take chemical defenses, for one. Many insects have poisonous or bad-tasting chemicals in their bodies. Some, like bees and wasps, can sting. Others spit or shoot acid at their foes, or they release foul-smelling chemicals.

Mimicry is also a widespread defense. Butterflies often mimic each other's color patterns for protection. There are insects that look like spiders, and spiders that look like insects. Some insects have false faces with real-looking eyes (see pages 46–47) And there are insects that use camouflage to hide in plain sight by resembling leaves, sticks, or other things in their environment. Additional adaptations that protect insects include spines, horns, sharp mandibles, and a thick exoskeleton.

Running, jumping, wriggling, flying away, and hiding are other ways insects avoid being eaten. If insects can't find hideouts, some will make their own by rolling leaves or creating other forms of shelter. Some insects confront their enemies by fighting them. In a pinch, others even shed appendages—the monkey slug caterpillar, for example, sheds its false legs—in order to escape.

Most impressive is how many insects use a variety of defenses. If one doesn't work, perhaps another will!

A bombardier beetle sprays a boiling-hot chemical when it feels threatened. It has excellent aim, and the chemical can cause intense pain.

The end of a wasp to avoid! The stinger is hollow and can inject its venom repeatedly. The painful sting has the effect of keeping potential enemies at bay.

A female clouded sulphur butterfly blends in with the leaves that surround her. Many insects rely on camouflage to be invisible to predators.

This saddleback caterpillar stings anything that comes too close to its hollow, venom-filled spines.

A green katydid resembles a leaf in color and pattern.

FALSE FACES

Birds are major predators of insects. But while hunting, birds can be spooked by anything resembling snakes or other bird-eating predators. If they don't react quickly, they might be eaten themselves! Insects have evolved ways to take advantage of this fear in birds and other animals that hunt using their sense of sight. Some insects have false faces with fake eyes, and some have eyespots that create the appearance of a spooky face staring back at you. Birds are easily startled by such false faces or eyes, giving the insect another chance to survive. Some false faces, however, may not be adaptations, but chance patterns that we mistakenly interpret as faces.

A spicebush swallowtail caterpillar's real head is tucked underneath the black line that looks like a mouth. The false eyes, complete with eyeshine, seem real.

The comical face on the back of this shield bug may not be a real adaptation to frighten predators, but its coloration may warn that it's toxic.

The eyed click beetle's false eyes can make potential predators hesitate to attack. But if attacked, it is able to jump to escape.

The io moth normally has its hind wings covered while it rests. If a bird approaches, it lifts its forewings to expose giant fake eyes.

The pupa of the *Dynastor darius* butterfly mimics a viper. It has a wide, false snake-shaped head with false snakelike eyes.

The oleander hawk-moth caterpillar has a pair of false eyes in a fold on its back. When disturbed (above), it tucks its head down and flashes its huge false eyes. When at rest (left), its false eyes are half closed.

THE SILK MAKERS

These silkworm caterpillars are encouraged to make silk cocoons in small cubicles. People use the cocoons' threads to make fabric.

Spiders spin silk threads for webs. But did you know that, at some point in their lives, many insects make silk threads too? The silk is a liquid inside the silk glands of insects and spiders, but when it is secreted from the glands and exposed to air, it dries into silk strands. Both insects and spiders use silk threads for many purposes, such as for making cocoons, traps, safe havens, drag lines, coverings for their eggs, and support structures. They also use silk for molting, wrapping prey, and ballooning (using the wind to blow them to another location).

Silk is a natural fiber composed of proteins. It is exceptionally strong and elastic. The larvae of most butterflies and moths and various other insects secrete silk from spinnerets below the mouth. But insects called web-spinners secrete silk from glands in their front legs. They work together to make their homes of silken tunnels and sheets on tree trunks, rocks, and leaf litter.

These ties are made from the unwound cocoons of the silk moth. The silk threads are dyed and woven into fabric.

10 COOL INSECT SILK MAKERS

MOTH LARVAE

WEBSPINNER NYMPHS

CERTAIN WASP AND BEE LARVAE

RASPY CRICKETS

FUNGUS GNAT LARVAE

WEAVER ANT LARVAE

CADDISFLY LARVAE

LACEWING EGG STALKS

BLACK FLY LARVAE

BUTTERFLY LARVAE

MIGRATION

A number of animals—many birds, some whales, African elephants, and caribou—migrate, and so do insects. Insects that migrate include Australia's Bogong moths, and many species of dragonflies, beetles, and butterflies, such as the well-known monarch. As with other animals, reasons that insects migrate include escaping drought or cold and finding food.

One of life's big mysteries has been exactly how animals migrate. When monarchs migrate, they use the sun as a compass. But the sun changes position in the sky over the day. Despite this, monarchs are able to keep flying in a particular direction. Scientists have been trying to learn how this happens. They have discovered a molecular process in the butterfly's antennae that compensates for the sun's shifting position.

Scientists also think that monarchs might use a magnetic compass that informs them where to go. Monarchs have a mineral in their bodies called magnetite. This mineral is the most magnetic on Earth. It's found not just in monarchs, but also in some other insects—such as bees, dragonflies, termites, and grasshoppers—as well as in migrating birds. It appears to play a role in insect migration, and scientists are actively researching this possibility.

Migration routes shown are some of the longer examples for the particular species.
ARCTIC OCEAN
Diamondback Moth
Hoverfly
ASIA
EUROPE
Painted Lady Butterfly
Hummingbird Hawk-moth
Armyworm Moth
PACIFIC OCEAN
AFRICA
Brown Planthopper
Desert Locust
Dark Blue Tiger Moth
EQUATOR
Globe Skimmer Dragonfly
INDIAN OCEAN
AUSTRALIA
Madagascan Sunset Moth
Bogong Moth
SOUTHERN OCEAN
ANTARCTICA

INSECTS AS PESTS

About one percent of insects are considered serious pests, yet their effect is impossible to ignore. Insect pests damage crops, eat wooden structures, sting, bite, ruin lawns and gardens, and make loud noises.

Lice, bedbugs, fleas, some flies, and some mosquitoes are pests—taking blood meals and leaving irritating rashes and bites. And some mosquitoes can endanger human health by carrying diseases like malaria. Malaria is a serious parasitic disease that affects more than 240 million people around the world. About 600,000 people die from it each year.

Although ticks are commonly thought of as insects, they are actually arachnids like scorpions, spiders, and mites. They also bite and can transmit microorganisms that cause human disease (such as Lyme disease and Rocky Mountain spotted fever). Chiggers, also related to spiders, can transmit illness, and they cause serious itching and leave red welts.

Locusts are grasshoppers that change their behavior and form huge swarms. "Plagues" of locusts can darken the sky as they fly into an area, and then eat everything in sight before moving on. The desert locust has such a reputation in drier parts of Africa.

Pest management has become a huge industry in which professional entomologists try to control the numbers of certain insect species. One means of controlling insect pests without poisoning the environment with pesticides is through biological pest control. Living organisms like predators and parasites are employed to do the job. Entomologists also help to protect species that are not pests.

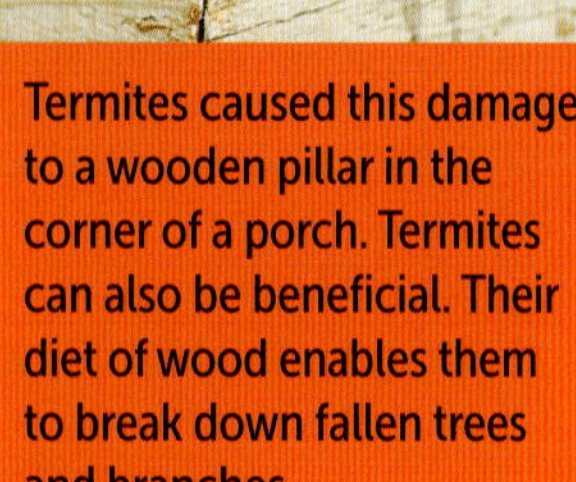

Termites caused this damage to a wooden pillar in the corner of a porch. Termites can also be beneficial. Their diet of wood enables them to break down fallen trees and branches.

Locusts travel in swarms, dropping into an area in huge numbers. They eat all plants in sight—including crops—before moving on to other areas. All grasshoppers start out as solitary, but only certain species are capable of becoming locusts. The change happens when grasshopper populations become very dense.

Body lice are one type of insect pest that especially affects people with limited access to bathing or clean clothes. The lice cause intense itching and might also transmit diseases such as typhus.

THE THREAT OF INSECT EXTINCTION

As human populations expand, people use more and more natural resources, and in the process they alter the natural environment. Most of Earth's land surface, about 83 percent, has been altered by humans. As a consequence of our activities, certain animals, including insects, have become extinct—which means they will never be seen again. And many other animals are in danger of extinction right now. Scientists estimate that many insects are disappearing even before they are discovered and named!

Extinction isn't the only threat facing insects. Threat of insect decline, which is a large drop in the number of individual insects around the world, is also a major threat. Such a decline would mean the loss of food crops, less control of insect pests, less food for many other animals, and more.

The aim of conservation is to preserve and protect animals and plants, their natural environments, and the ecosystems they live in. And where natural areas have been damaged, people are making efforts to restore them to their previously healthy condition.

When we help animals, plants, and the environment, we help ourselves, too!

As Harvard biologist E. O. Wilson once wrote, **"SO IMPORTANT ARE INSECTS** and other land-dwelling arthropods that **IF ALL WERE TO DISAPPEAR, HUMANITY PROBABLY COULD NOT LAST** more than a few months."

Insect species are most diverse in tropical rainforests. But every year, catastrophic fires burn down huge areas of rainforest and bring about the loss of lives and habitats. One problem facing us is how to manage land in order to maintain biodiversity and a healthy ecosystem.

10 CHALLENGES INSECTS FACE

WATER POLLUTION

DEFORESTATION

AIR POLLUTION

INDUSTRIAL WASTE (IN WATER)

CLIMATE CHANGE (FLOODING)

BUILDING CONSTRUCTION

INDUSTRIAL WASTE (ON LAND)

CLIMATE CHANGE (DROUGHT)

HABITAT DEGRADATION

OVERUSE OF PESTICIDES

SIMPLE
METAMORPHOSIS

BALLOON-WINGED KATYDID NYMPH

A KATYDID NYMPH PERCHING ON A FLOWER BUD

AN ASSASSIN BUG NYMPH SLIDING OUT OF ITS OLD EXOSKELETON

A NEWLY EMERGED SKIMMER DRAGONFLY HANGING FROM ITS NYMPHAL EXOSKELETON

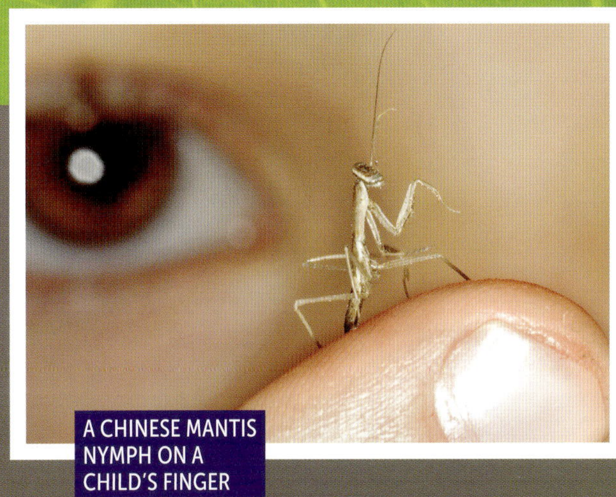

A CHINESE MANTIS NYMPH ON A CHILD'S FINGER

INSECT ORDERS

Young insects, called nymphs, undergo simple metamorphosis as they grow up, which means they often look like miniature versions of the adult insects they will become. Many, but not all, insects with this form of metamorphosis will develop wings. The ones that will have wings have wing buds visible on their backs while they're nymphs.

Insects are in the kingdom Animalia, the phylum Arthropoda, and the class Insecta. On these two pages, you'll find all the different orders of insects with simple metamorphosis. The scientific name for the order is noted below the common name and is followed by its pronunciation. The figures below it are estimates of the number of species in that order that have already been named and described. To find out about some of the different insects within an order, just turn to the pages noted.

There are three orders with insects that undergo simple metamorphosis that aren't included in the profiles that start on page 60. They are:

BOOKLICE AND BARKLICE
Psocodea
so · CODE · ee · ah
About 5,500 species of small, scavenging insects

WEBSPINNERS
Embioptera
em · bee · OP · ter · uh
About 400 described species of insects that spin silk from glands on their legs and live inside silk structures

ANGEL INSECTS
Zoraptera
zor · APP · ter · uh
About 35 species of tiny, termite-like insects that live in rotting wood

MAYFLIES
Ephemeroptera
ih · FEM · uh · ROP · ter · uh

About 3,500 species
pages 60–61

EARWIGS
Dermaptera
der · MAP · ter · uh

About 2,000 species
pages 72–73

ICEBUGS
Notoptera (also called *Grylloblattodea*)
no · TOP · ter · uh

About 30 species
pages 74–75

STONEFLIES
Plecoptera
pleh · COP · ter · uh

About 3,700 species
pages 76–77

DRAGONFLIES AND DAMSELFLIES
Odonata
oh · duh · NA · ta

About 6,300 species
pages 62–71

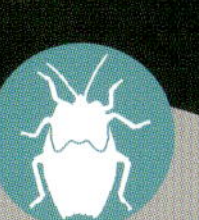

CRICKETS, GRASSHOPPERS, AND KATYDIDS
Orthoptera
or · THOP · tur · uh

About 30,000 species
pages 84–93

LEAF INSECTS AND STICK INSECTS
Phasmatodea
faz · ma · TOE · dee · uh

About 3,000 species
pages 78–83

MANTISES
Mantodea
man · TOE · dee · uh

About 2,400 species
pages 94–97

TERMITES AND COCKROACHES
Blattodea
blat · TOE · dee · uh

About 6,600 species
pages 98–101

LICE
Phthiraptera
THIR · AP · ter · uh

About 5,000 species
pages 102–103

THRIPS
Thysanoptera
thigh · san · OP · ter · uh

About 6,200 species
pages 104–105

TRUE BUGS
Hemiptera
hem · IP · tur · uh

About 82,000 species
pages 106–141

Mayflies are easily recognized by their long, threadlike tails. This adult green drake mayfly has long, triangular-shaped forewings and much smaller hind wings. It holds its wings upright when resting.

That's Fact-tastic!
IN GERMAN, the common name for mayflies is EINTAGSFLIEGEN. The word means "ONE-DAY FLIES."

GREEN DRAKE MAYFLY
FAMILY EPHEMERIDAE

Mayflies belong to a group of insects that first appeared between 323 and 299 million years ago. That makes them one of the world's oldest insects! In spite of their longevity as a group, mayflies have an incredibly short life span. Adult members of many species, like the green drake, live only one day! Although many mayflies live only a short time as adults, they can spend more than two years as nymphs. During this time, they go through several molts, maturing a bit each time. Eventually, they develop wings and soon become adults.

Green drakes spend their brief adult life in search of a mate so that they can reproduce. Males and females join together in large swarms that form over bodies of water such as lakes and rivers. After mating, the female deposits her fertilized eggs on the surface of the water. The mating process takes so much energy that the mayflies die soon afterward.

FACTS

COMMON NAME Green drake

SCIENTIFIC NAME *Ephemera danica* / Family: Ephemeridae

SIZE Wingspan up to 1.5 inches (38 mm)

WINGS Yes

FOOD Adult: none / Nymph: tiny, dead animals; algae floating in the water

HABITAT Lakes and rivers with sandy or gravel bottoms

RANGE Throughout Europe

Mayflies, like the group shown here swarming on the water's surface, often **EMERGE AROUND THE SAME TIME.** After their last molt, they **MATE AND DIE.**

GIANT DARNER DRAGONFLY

FAMILY AESHNIDAE

Darners include some of the world's largest dragonflies. Among them is the giant darner, which grows up to five inches (127 mm) long and has a wingspan that's about the length of its body.

Darners are fierce predators—even as nymphs. They'll attack just about anything they can snatch, including organisms much bigger than they are. This includes aquatic insects, worms, fish, and small frogs.

How does a nymph seize a big meal? It relies mainly on its labium, an extendible jaw underneath its head. When the nymph gets close enough to its prey, it shoots its labium forward. Hooks on the labium snare the victim and keep it from escaping. The nymph then retracts its labium, dragging the prey to its mouth. *Chomp!*

FACTS

COMMON NAME Giant darner

SCIENTIFIC NAME *Anax walsinghami* / Family: Aeshnidae

SIZE Wingspan up to 5 inches (127 mm)

WINGS Yes

FOOD Adult: small insects / Nymph: aquatic insects, small tadpoles, and fish

HABITAT Streams, ponds, marshes

RANGE Southwestern United States, western Mexico, and Honduras

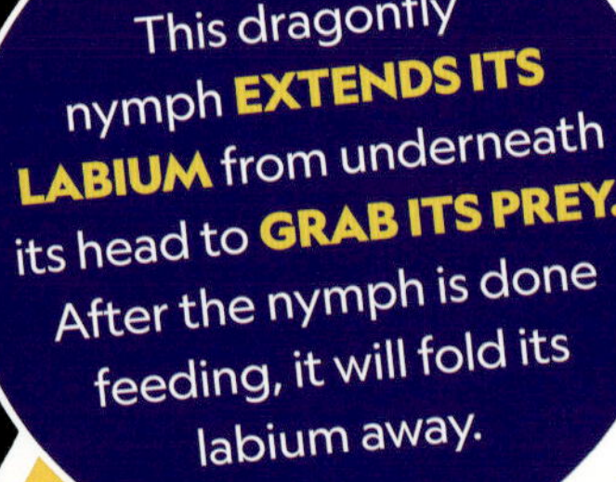

A dragonfly's wings contain many veins. The insect's heart pumps blood into its wings through these veins.

That's **Fact-tastic!**

THREE HUNDRED MILLION YEARS ago dragonflies were about **FIVE TIMES LARGER** than those today. Their wings measured about **28 INCHES** (70 cm) **FROM TIP TO TIP.** That is **GREATER THAN** the wingspan of **SOME PARROTS!**

That's
Fact-tastic!
MALE Kirby's
dropwing skimmers
are a BRIGHT
ORANGE-RED. By
contrast, FEMALES
ARE YELLOW.

KIRBY'S DROPWING SKIMMER
FAMILY LIBELLULIDAE

Currently, there are 13 known families of dragonflies. The largest family is made up of about 1,000 species, including Kirby's dropwing skimmer.

Some dragonflies catch their prey while flying, but skimmers prefer to do most of their hunting from a perch. They hang out on objects such as twigs, leaf stalks, and branches, from which they scan the area for food. When their prey is in close range, they dart out to grab the victim, then return to their perch to eat.

When the male skimmer isn't hunting, it takes flight. It patrols the area for other male dragonflies, which it considers a threat to its food supply, as well as competition for mates.

FACTS

COMMON NAME Kirby's dropwing skimmer

SCIENTIFIC NAME *Trithemis kirbyi* / Family: Libellulidae

SIZE 1.3–1.5 inches (35–38 mm)

WINGS Yes

FOOD Adult: small insects / Nymph: aquatic insects and small aquatic animals

HABITAT Streams, rivers, and pools in savanna, woodland, or bush

RANGE Africa, southern Europe, Middle East, Indian Ocean islands, and southern Asia

Globe skimmers (*Plata flavescens*) **MIGRATE 11,200 MILES** (18,000 km) over the Indian Ocean each year. **IT TAKES SEVERAL GENERATIONS TO DO THIS.** An individual can fly some 3,700 miles (5,955 km)!

65

DRAGONFLIES GALLERY

Dragonflies have fascinated people for centuries. Their brightly colored bodies have inspired works of art, while their sewing-needle shape has given rise to strange legends. According to one tale, dragonflies would sew up the mouths of people who told lies! But in reality, dragonflies are harmless to people. In fact, they eat insects such as mosquitoes and midges, which can be pests to humans.

Dragonflies have excellent vision. They have two large compound eyes that are about half the size of their heads. The eyes are sensitive to motion, so when hunting for food, dragonflies can easily follow a quick-flying insect. Other dragonflies will wait for their prey to come to them. Dragonfly nymphs are meat-eaters too, but their diet comes from what they find in their aquatic environment.

These insects are diverse and come in many different shapes, sizes, and colors. Want to know more? Check out the six examples shown on these pages.

A Halloween pennant skimmer perches on a plant.

This migrant hawker, with its bright blue-and-brown body, can be found in parts of Europe and Asia.

The Indian pied paddy skimmer has a striking wing pattern, but it isn't a strong flier. These dragonflies rarely stray from their breeding sites—usually paddy fields and streams.

Southern darters forming a mating wheel. The red one is the male.

A dragonfly's two large compound eyes consist of thousands of tiny facets that help it see clearly. Two simple eyes visible below them detect light and dark.

Just because predators can easily spot brightly colored dragonflies doesn't mean that they can catch them. Many dragonflies are speedy and can outfly predatory birds.

That's Fact-tastic!

The male helicopter damselfly is **TERRITORIAL** and **WILL DEFEND A TREE HOLE** in his territory from other males. A male **WILL NOT PERMIT A FEMALE TO LAY HER EGGS IN HIS TREE HOLE** unless she mates with him first.

HELICOPTER DAMSELFLY
FAMILY PSEUDOSTIGMATIDAE

Helicopter damselflies are cool to encounter while walking through a tropical rainforest in Central or South America. These giant insects seem to fly in slow motion as they appear in a beam of sunlight through a gap in the tree canopy. When the sunlight hits the damselfly, the yellow spots on the ends of its long, transparent wings seem to bounce up and down.

Damselflies are related to dragonflies, but unlike dragonflies, they close their wings when they come to rest. The helicopter damselfly has a unique diet. It flies up to a spiderweb and plucks the spider right out of the web. It might even take the spider's wrapped prey too.

These damselflies also visit small bodies of water—in tree holes and in the cup formed by the leaves of certain plants, like tank bromeliads. The female lays her eggs there, and the naiads (nymphs) live in the water, feeding on various insects and even on frog tadpoles.

FACTS

OTHER COMMON NAMES Giant damselfly, forest giant

SCIENTIFIC NAME Family: Pseudostigmatidae

SIZE Wingspan up to 7.5 inches (190 mm)

WINGS Yes

FOOD Adult: spiders and spider prey / Naiad: mosquito larvae, flies, tadpoles, and other naiads

HABITAT Tropical habitats; naiads in water-filled tree holes and bromeliads

RANGE Mexico, Central America, and tropical parts of South America

A female helicopter damselfly, *Megaloprepus caerulatus*, **LAYS HER EGGS IN A TREE HOLE.**

COMMON BLUE DAMSELFLY
FAMILY COENAGRIONIDAE

Common blue damselflies, like other dragonflies and damselflies, start their lives as nymphs in fresh water. As youngsters, they feed on small aquatic animals. They have a lower lip that shoots out to grab their prey. When temperatures drop at the start of winter, the nymphs undergo diapause. That means they are able to become inactive until next spring. Nymphs that experience diapause are typically larger when they become adults because they have more time to grow than nymphs that complete their metamorphosis all in one season.

As adults, common blue damselflies catch their prey in flight. After mating, a pair will stay together and the male will hang onto the female and guard her while she lays her eggs on plants underwater.

Pesticides that people use to kill unwanted insects can have a bad effect on beneficial insects. Damselfly nymphs are especially sensitive to the chemicals, and it hinders their ability to survive and reproduce. Pesticides also get into fresh water through runoff and by spraying to get rid of mosquitoes.

FACTS

OTHER COMMON NAMES Northern bluet, common bluet

SCIENTIFIC NAME *Enallagma cyathigerum* / Family: Coenagrionidae

SIZE 1.3 inches (32 mm)

WINGS Yes

FOOD Adult: mostly flies, mosquitoes, and moths / Naiad: mosquito larvae and other small aquatic insects

HABITAT Near bodies of fresh water: ponds, streams, lakes, puddles

RANGE United States, Canada, Great Britain, Sweden, Norway, Finland, Russia, South Korea, and other northern countries

Two damselflies forming a mating wheel. **THE INDIVIDUAL ON THE RIGHT IS THE FEMALE.**

EARWIG
ORDER DERMAPTERA

According to a common myth, earwigs crawl into the ears of people sleeping outdoors, then burrow into their brains and kill them. Not true!

There are some 2,000 species of earwigs. Their short, leatherlike forewings give this order its name, which means "skin wings." At their tail end, many earwigs have two long pincers. The pincers are used during courtship and for capturing prey, defending against predators, and folding and unfolding their membranous hind wings.

After most female insects lay eggs, their parental responsibility to the next generation is over. However, some female earwigs care for their eggs and young nymphs. They clean the eggs regularly to prevent fungal growth, and they defend their young from predators. As the young grow up, they go through four to six molts. The final molt results in an adult.

FACTS

COMMON NAME Earwig

SCIENTIFIC NAME Order: Dermaptera

SIZE The common earwig, *Forficula auricularia*, grows up to 0.75 inch (20 mm)

WINGS Short forewings, membranous hind wings for flying; some species are wingless

FOOD Adult and nymph: flowers, leaves, fruits, aphids, spiders, insect eggs, and mold

HABITAT In soil, crevices, and debris

RANGE The Americas, Africa, Europe, Asia, Australia, and New Zealand

ICEBUG
FAMILY GRYLLOBLATTIDAE

You'd think that insects would avoid really cold places. But there are a few that defy expectations—the icebugs. For them, the ideal temperature is close to freezing, between 33.8° and 37.4°F (1° and 3°C), but they can tolerate lower temperatures too. Icebugs are extremophiles—organisms that, along with water bears and certain bacteria, live under extreme environmental conditions. When it gets too cold for icebugs, they burrow under snow packs, under rocks, and in other places so they don't freeze. Their bodies have a built-in kind of antifreeze that lowers their freezing temperature.

Icebugs are wingless and have chewing mouthparts. They are active at night and can be seen scrambling out onto snow fields to feed on frozen insects.

FACTS

OTHER COMMON NAMES Ice crawler, rock crawler

SCIENTIFIC NAME Family: Grylloblattidae

SIZE 0.7–1.5 inches (17–38 mm)

WINGS No

FOOD Adult and nymph: other insects and plant material

HABITAT Cold areas, usually in mountains, under rocks, in caves, on leaf litter

RANGE Japan, China, Korea, eastern Siberia, and western North America

Icebugs have adapted to live in such cold environments that **IF YOU PUT ONE IN YOUR HAND, IT WILL COOK!** The proteins in their bodies break down at room temperature.

STONEFLY
ORDER PLECOPTERA

Stoneflies are poor fliers, so they can't travel very far. As a result, these insects have to come up with creative ways to meet other members of their species.

To find a mate, a male stonefly will drum up some noise—literally. The male produces a series of vibrations, called "drumming," by tapping, rubbing, or scraping his abdomen on a rock or log. Some males even do push-ups!

The drumming vibrations travel through the rock or log and get the attention of any female nearby. If the female is interested, she responds by drumming back. The two stoneflies continue to communicate in this way until they find each other.

COMMON NAME Stonefly

SCIENTIFIC NAME Order: Plecoptera

SIZE 0.25–2 inches (6–50 mm)

WINGS Some species are wingless

FOOD Adult: some species feed on pollen, lichen, and nectar / Nymph: plant matter or small aquatic animals, depending on species

HABITAT On rocks or logs near rivers and streams

RANGE Worldwide except Antarctica

The larvae of stoneflies **CAN'T SURVIVE IN POLLUTED WATERS.** So their presence in streams or rivers suggests that the **QUALITY OF THE WATER IS GOOD.**

LEAF INSECT
FAMILY PHYLLIIDAE

Leaf insects are some of the most remarkable examples of camouflage. Together with the walking sticks, they make up the order Phasmatodea, which comes from the Greek word *phasma,* meaning phantom or ghost.

Leaf insects mimic leaves so convincingly that you can look right at one on a branch and not see that it's an insect. Various species take on the color of live green leaves or dead or dying ones. Most have what looks exactly like leaf veins on their abdomen. Some appear to have bite marks on their "leaf" edges. These insects even sway back and forth, resembling a leaf in the wind.

FACTS

OTHER COMMON NAME Walking leaf

SCIENTIFIC NAME Family: Phylliidae

SIZE 2–4 inches (50–100 mm)

WINGS Yes, but only the hind wings are used by the males to fly

FOOD Adult and nymph: leaves

HABITAT Tropical forests

RANGE India to Fiji islands, and expanding into Micronesia

One of the oldest known leaf insect fossils is **47 MILLION YEARS OLD.** It was found in Germany.

CHAN'S MEGASTICK
FAMILY PHASMATIDAE

Chan's megastick is a mega-size stick insect. It is the longest known insect in the world, measuring 22.3 inches (566 mm) with its legs outstretched. That's almost two feet! It was named after the person who discovered it. Its body is pencil-thin and resembles a bamboo shoot. With such remarkable camouflage, it can seem invisible to birds and other predators.

Most Chan's megasticks live in tropical and sub-tropical areas. They sleep during the day and eat leaves at night.

Stick insects generally flick their eggs in the air so the eggs can drop to the ground. The megastick's eggs are unique. They are flat, lightweight, and have little wings to help them drift and scatter in the wind.

FACTS

COMMON NAME Chan's megastick

SCIENTIFIC NAME *Phobaeticus chani* / Family: Phasmatidae

SIZE With legs outstretched, 22.3 inches (566 mm) / Body alone 14 inches (355 mm)

WINGS Yes

FOOD Adult and nymph: leaves

HABITAT Rainforest

RANGE State of Sabah on the island of Borneo

Many stick insects can **REPRODUCE WITHOUT MATING.** The female produces **EGGS THAT ARE CLONES** of herself. In fact, scientists have been **UNABLE TO FIND EVEN ONE MALE** in certain species of stick insects!

MANGA METALLIC STICK INSECT
FAMILY PHASMATIDAE

The manga metallic stick insect is so rare, it is known from only one small location on the African island of Madagascar. The males are spectacular, having shiny turquoise blue bodies with orange accents and red wings. (The word "manga" means "blue" in the Malagasy language.) The females and juveniles, however, are hard to find—they have brownish branch-like coloration. Their camouflage helps them blend in with their environment. It is likely that females prefer males with bright coloration. Male nymphs develop the bright colors when they get old enough to mate.

This stick insect can protect itself from predators by rubbing its second pair of wings together to make loud grating or sizzling sounds. This form of noise-making is called stridulation, and is common in various arthropods. They can also deter preda-tors by secreting a substance from glands in their neck that acts as a repellent.

Females are larger than males, and they move around a lot less. After mating, the female lays many eggs and tosses them into surrounding vegetation. Originally collected in 2007, this species was misidentified as another species. Once scientists were able to prove it was a unique species, they published the description and new name in 2019.

Another species from Madagascar, the **MALAGASY STICK INSECT** (*Achrioptera fallax*) **ALSO HAS METALLIC BLUE MALES AND CAMOUFLAGED FEMALES.** The females lay their eggs in the soil, where they incubate for six to nine months.

MOLE CRICKET
FAMILY GRYLLOTALPIDAE

If you hear loud chirping on a spring night, you might be listening to the sound of a mole cricket. Male mole crickets chirp by rubbing two parts of their body together. For instance, the European mole cricket rubs the specialized veins that are on the tip of each of its forewings. These veins are called a "harp."

As the mole cricket plays its harp, the chirping sound travels through the air and is detected by a female nearby. If she likes the song, she'll find the male and mate with him. Typically, females prefer songs that have a higher pitch. This indicates that the male cricket is larger and will likely be a more suitable mate.

To ensure that his chirps travel far enough to reach any females in the area, the male mole cricket performs a little trick. He produces his chirps while inside a special burrow. The burrow acts like a megaphone, amplifying the sound of
the chirps!

FACTS

OTHER COMMON NAME European mole cricket

SCIENTIFIC NAME *Gryllotalpa gryllotalpa* / Family: Gryllotalpidae

SIZE 1.4–1.8 inches (35–46 mm)

WINGS Yes

FOOD Adult: roots and stems of plants; worms; larvae of other insects / Nymph: soil invertebrates and plant material

HABITAT Damp, rich soils; floodplains; vegetable gardens

RANGE Europe and United States

Male mole crickets have **SPADE-LIKE FORELEGS, WHICH THEY USE TO DIG THEIR SPECIALIZED BURROW.** The forelegs are powerful and can scoop out dirt and push it to the surface quickly.

EASTERN LUBBER
FAMILY ACRIDIDAE

Many grasshoppers rely on their jumping abilities to escape predators. But the eastern lubber isn't a very good hopper. Its large size and short wings make this insect a slow, clumsy mover. Still, the lubber isn't easy prey. It has a few special tricks to ward off enemies.

When eastern lubbers are nymphs (photo below), they move around in large groups. This makes them look like one large insect, which can intimidate some potential predators.

When attacked, the adult lubber sprays out a foamy brown liquid made from a mixture of chemicals and recently digested plant material.

The lubber might also make sound effects when attacked. It pushes air out of tiny holes inside its thorax. The result is a loud hissing sound that can startle some predators.

FACTS

COMMON NAME Eastern lubber

SCIENTIFIC NAME *Romalea guttata* / Family: Acrididae

SIZE 2–3.5 inches (50–90 mm)

WINGS Yes

FOOD Adult and nymph: plants

HABITAT Woodland and fields

RANGE Southeastern and south-central United States

The eastern lubber's bright **ORANGE, YELLOW, AND BLACK PATTERN ACTS AS A WARNING SIGN.** It lets predators know that **IT'S TOXIC.** Predators that don't heed the warning get a **BAD CASE OF INDIGESTION** when they eat the lubber!

That's
Fact-tastic!

Unlike most
grasshoppers, blue-
winged grasshoppers
DON'T MAKE
SNAPPING, CRACKLING,
OR BUZZING SOUNDS
when in flight.

BLUE-WINGED GRASSHOPPER

FAMILY ACRIDIDAE

Some grasshoppers use color to confuse their predators. Take, for instance, the blue-winged grasshopper. At rest, this insect is a mottled brown (photo below). But when it takes flight, the grasshopper's hind wings spread open to reveal a bright shade of blue.

The blue appearance can attract the attention of predators. Some birds may even mistake the airborne grasshopper for a fluttering butterfly. But when it is chased, the grasshopper shuts its wings and drops to the ground. The blue is no longer visible—and neither is the grasshopper to its potential attacker. Camouflaged against the ground, the blue-winged grasshopper can be sitting just a few feet from its predator without being detected!

FACTS

COMMON NAME Blue-winged grasshopper

SCIENTIFIC NAME *Oedipoda caerulescens* / Family: Acrididae

SIZE 0.6–1.1 inches (15–28 mm)

WINGS Yes

FOOD Adult and nymph: plants such as grasses

HABITAT Dunes, heath, grasslands

RANGE Europe, North Africa, and Asia

GRASSHOPPERS GALLERY

In the order Orthoptera, most of what we call "grasshoppers" have short antennae. The others—katydids, crickets, and wetas—have long antennae, and are sometimes called long-horned grasshoppers because their antennae are longer than their bodies. Grasshopper antennae collect chemical signals in the air and help to locate plants on which the grasshoppers feed.

Many grasshoppers have a knack for jumping great distances. A grasshopper can cover 20 times its body length in just one hop.

To jump, grasshoppers rely on powerful muscles in their long hind legs and a springlike mechanism in their knees. These help propel the grasshopper upward and forward at high speed.

Like many insects, grasshoppers come in different colors. A few are even pink! Set your sights on these six colorful creatures.

When conditions get crowded, some grasshoppers become locusts, like this desert locust. They can fly long distances in swarms, devastating fields of crops along the way.

Some grasshoppers, like this army hopper, have mottled bodies that help them blend in with their environment.

A gaudy grasshopper rests on blades of grass but is poised to hop at any moment.

The nymphs of the differential grasshopper, like the adults, feed on many different plants, including grasses, soybeans, and clovers.

Eastern lubber grasshopper nymphs form a large group after hatching.

Though most grasshoppers are green or brown, some—like this pink nymph—are much brighter. Pink grasshoppers are rare, most likely because they are easy for predators to spot.

CONEHEAD KATYDID
SUBFAMILY COPIPHORINAE

Can you spot the conehead katydid? At first glance, it looks like a leaf. That's because the conehead katydid's appearance helps it to blend in against a leafy background. This grasshopper-like insect usually has a cone on top of its head. In conehead species that live in the grasslands, the cone helps to camouflage the insect among the grasses. In other environments, these pointy cones may help protect the katydid from bats.

At night, conehead katydids can draw a bit of attention to themselves. Some species make loud chirping sounds, and even dance, to attract mates. One species of conehead produce the loudest songs in North America. It can be heard as far away as a third of a mile.

FACTS

COMMON NAME	Conehead katydid
SCIENTIFIC NAME	Subfamily: Copiphorinae
SIZE	0.9–2.9 inches (24–74 mm)
WINGS	Yes
FOOD	Adult and nymph: seeds, fruit, and small invertebrates
HABITAT	Rainforests, grasslands
RANGE	Worldwide; mostly tropical and sub-tropical regions

It's hard to spot this conehead katydid in the wild because it **LOOKS EXACTLY LIKE A LEAF!**

ORTHOPTERA KATYDIDS

Conehead katydids get their common name from the round or pointed cone at the top of their heads. This particular species, Copiphora rhinoceros, is known as the rhinoceros spearbearer for obvious reasons.

That's Fact-tastic!
How do katydids hear? They HAVE AN EAR IN EACH FORELEG. Their inner ears are surprisingly SIMILAR TO OUR OWN EARS.

That's
Fact-tastic!

The praying mantis is the
STATE INSECT OF CONNECTICUT—
even though it's not native to the
U.S. state. The praying mantis is
ORIGINALLY FROM NORTHERN
AFRICA, SOUTHERN EUROPE,
AND PARTS OF ASIA. Experts
believe that the insect was
ACCIDENTALLY SHIPPED TO
NORTH AMERICA with some
nursery plants in 1899.

PRAYING MANTIS
FAMILY MANTIDAE

The praying mantis is named for its long forelimbs, which the insect holds folded in front of its body as if praying. However, this mantis isn't praying—it's *preying*!

The mantis sits motionless on a plant, waiting for a juicy insect such as a fly or cricket to come by. Usually, the prey has no idea what's about to happen because it can't detect the predator. That's because the mantis's body blends in with the plant it's sitting on.

When the prey is in close range, the mantis strikes. Its front legs shoot out to seize the insect. These legs are covered with spikes, allowing the mantis to get a firm grip on the struggling prey as it begins to chomp away on it.

FACTS

OTHER COMMON NAME European mantis

SCIENTIFIC NAME *Mantis religiosa* / Family: Mantidae

SIZE 2–3 inches (50–75 mm)

WINGS Yes

FOOD Adult: insects such as flies, crickets, and mosquitoes / Nymph: small insects and, sometimes, each other

HABITAT Meadows, fields, gardens, pastures, and roadsides

RANGE Europe, North America, Asia, and Africa

This praying mantis is **SINKING ITS MANDIBLES** into a grasshopper.

MANTISES GALLERY

Not all mantises are green or brown like the praying mantis. Depending on the species, these masters of disguise come in many colors, including pink and white, which make them look like flowers. Some species in Africa can change their color. They are bright green in the rainy season, when their environment is lush with green plants. They turn brown in the dry season, when most of these plants shrivel and die. This change of color helps to camouflage them at any time of year.

Most mantises are loners. They can't live with other members of their species because they might eat them!

There are more than 2,400 species of mantises in the world. Here are a few for you to feast your eyes on.

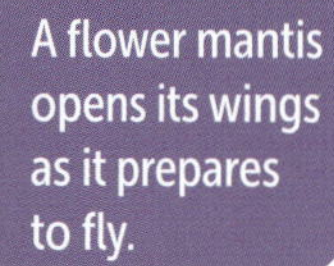

A flower mantis opens its wings as it prepares to fly.

The forelegs of a praying mantis have sharp spikes. The mantis uses them to pin its prey and to scratch the eyes of some of its attackers (like birds).

In this photo, the mantis's front legs are raised in a defensive posture.

When a mantis feels threatened, it strikes a defensive pose. In this case, it fans out its wings to seem larger—and even more intimidating—than it already is.

A praying mantis's vision plays an important role in hunting. The insect uses its large compound eyes to spot prey, and it can turn its head 180 degrees to see what's happening directly behind it.

This Malaysian orchid mantis can be hard to spot on similarly colored orchids. In this photo, everything that looks like a pink petal is a part of the mantis.

MAGNETIC TERMITE
FAMILY TERMITIDAE

Magnetic termites, like ants and other termites, live together in groups, or colonies. They are social insects, which means colony members perform different tasks. Even the nymphs of some species serve as workers: They help with finding food and maintaining the nest.

The magnetic termite makes mounds up to 13 feet (4 m) tall, and each colony has its own mound. This species of termite got its name from the way it constructs its flattened mound in a north–south direction. The termite has an internal compass—a sense of direction—that helps direct mound-building. In northern Australia, it's quite a sight to see a field full of mounds all oriented in the same direction. The thin shape and alignment of the mounds provides a stable, temperature-controlled structure for the termites to live in, even when their habitat is flooded for part of the year.

Many termites specialize in eating wood and dead plant material. The workers are responsible for digesting the food and then feeding it to the other members of the colony.

FACTS

OTHER COMMON NAME Compass termite

SCIENTIFIC NAME *Amitermes meridionalis* / Family: Termitidae

SIZE Soldier: 0.16–0.24 inch (4–6 mm)

WINGS Reproductives: yes; workers: no

FOOD Adult and nymph: dead wood and grasses

HABITAT Seasonally flooded savanna plains

RANGE Northern Australia

Aboriginal (Native) Australians make a **WIND INSTRUMENT** from thin **TREE TRUNKS THAT ARE HOLLOWED OUT BY TERMITES.** This traditional instrument, **THE DIDGERIDOO,** has been around for about 1,500 years. Some believe it's been used much longer.

Magnetic
termites—
adults and
nymphs

INDIAN DOMINO COCKROACH
FAMILY CORYDIIDAE

If there's such a thing as a cute cockroach, then the Indian domino cockroach would probably win the title. This roach is black with seven white spots on the hardened, leathery wings that cover its back. Hidden underneath the spotted wings is the roach's bright orange back. It typically doesn't show because the roaches do not fly.

An insect called the six-spot ground beetle (also called the domino beetle) lives in the same area as the domino cockroach. The beetle is large, black, has sharp mandibles, and has six white spots instead of seven. It can shoot a jet of stinging acid to protect itself from predators. The domino cockroach is thought to mimic the domino beetle. Looking a lot like the beetle helps give the roach some protection from predators. A hungry predator doesn't count the number of white spots!

FACTS

OTHER COMMON NAMES Desert cockroach, seven-spotted cockroach

SCIENTIFIC NAME *Therea petiveriana* / Family: Corydiidae

SIZE About 1.2 inches (30 mm)

WINGS Yes, but they do not use them to fly

FOOD Adult and nymph: rotting plants and poop

HABITAT Scrub forests

RANGE Sri Lanka and Southern India

THIS COCKROACH IS LAYING A SAC FULL OF EGGS. However, most species of cockroaches lay their eggs in sacs (or egg cases) in moist leaf litter. After a period of time, the nymphs emerge and will live underground until they become adults.

HEAD LOUSE
FAMILY PEDICULIDAE

Try not to scratch yourself as you read this page. If you're unlucky enough to get head lice, don't be embarrassed. You're in good company. Many people have been getting them for thousands of years. Just take measures to get rid of them as soon as possible.

Head lice are flightless insects that live exclusively on blood from people's scalps. A related subspecies (body lice) lives in clothes and feeds on other parts of a person's body. Head lice don't cause disease, but they are annoying and hard to get rid of. Without wings, head lice transfer from one person to another, usually by head-to-head contact. The adult louse glues its eggs, called nits, to individual strands of a person's hair near the scalp. The newly hatched nymphs look like miniature adults and also feed on the scalp.

Girls are more likely to get head lice than boys or adults are. Scientists are studying the reasons why.

FACTS

COMMON NAME Head louse

SCIENTIFIC NAME *Pediculus humanus* / Subspecies: *capitis* / Family: Pediculidae

SIZE 0.04–0.12 inch (1–3 mm)

WINGS No

FOOD Adult and nymph: human blood

HABITAT People's heads

RANGE Worldwide

THRIPS
ORDER THYSANOPTERA

Some thrips have a bad reputation. They can be crop pests, transmitting plant viruses and leaving scars on fruit, leaves, and flowers. But thrips do a lot of good, too. There are species that are predators of other insects and mites that damage crops. And thrips are major pollinators of certain tropical rainforest trees.

In Malaysia, Indonesia, and the Philippines, many of the tallest rainforest trees, called dipterocarps, produce huge displays of flowers (photo below), but at irregular intervals of two to 10 years. Dependent on the weather, they will flower only when the conditions are right—and when they do, it's spectacular. The main pollinators of these trees are thrips. They crawl around in the trees' flowers and get covered in pollen.

These thrips reproduce very fast. Their life cycle is complete in eight days. In short order, their increasing numbers are enough to fill vast canopies of flowering trees.

FACTS

OTHER COMMON NAMES Thunderfly, thunderbug

SCIENTIFIC NAME Order: Thysanoptera

SIZE 0.02–0.55 inch (0.5–14 mm)

WINGS Yes, feathery

FOOD Adult and nymph: plants, flowers, mites, insects, and fungal spores

HABITAT Varies

RANGE Worldwide

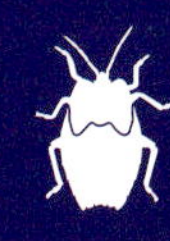

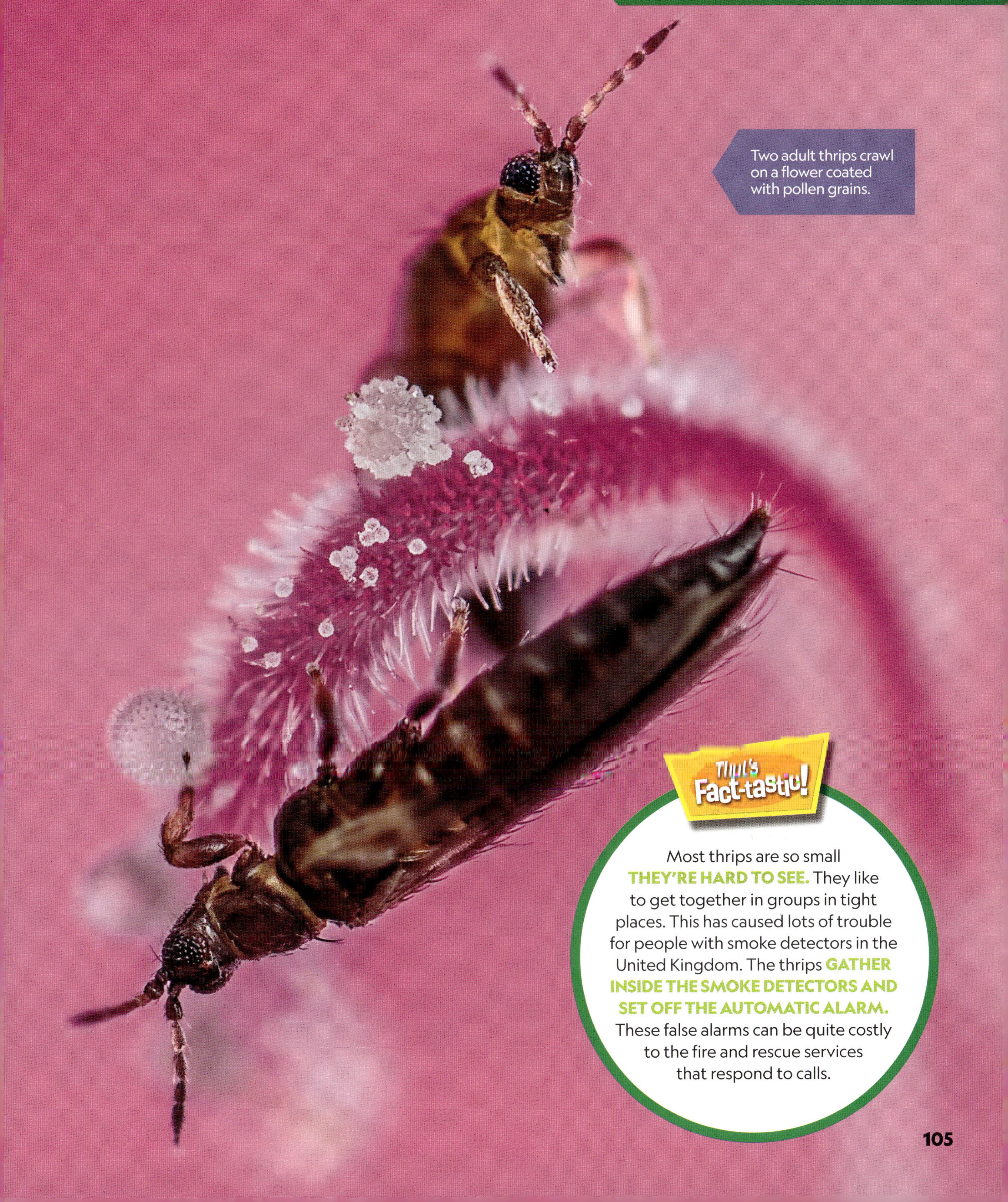

Two adult thrips crawl on a flower coated with pollen grains.

That's Fact-tastic!

Most thrips are so small **THEY'RE HARD TO SEE.** They like to get together in groups in tight places. This has caused lots of trouble for people with smoke detectors in the United Kingdom. The thrips **GATHER INSIDE THE SMOKE DETECTORS AND SET OFF THE AUTOMATIC ALARM.** These false alarms can be quite costly to the fire and rescue services that respond to calls.

GREEN GROCER
FAMILY CICADIDAE

You might not always see cicadas, but you can definitely hear them. The green grocer from the east coast of Australia is one of the loudest cicadas of all. It annoys human residents with its ear-shattering love songs every summer. Green is the predominant color of the adult cicadas. However, they come in other colors as well, depending on their diet and on the temperature under which the nymphs were raised.

The nymphs live underground, feeding on plant roots for about seven years. They emerge as adults in summer, and within a few short weeks they mate, lay eggs, and die.

Cicadas are widespread in temperate and tropical parts of the world with more than 3,000 known species, most having their own unique song. They cling to tree trunks and limbs and suck sap with their long proboscis.

FACTS

OTHER COMMON NAMES Yellow Monday, blue moon, chocolate soldier, masked devil

SCIENTIFIC NAME *Cyclochila australasiae* / Family: Cicadidae

SIZE 1.6 inches (40 mm) long, 4.3–5 inches (110–130 mm) wingspan

WINGS Yes

FOOD Adult: plant sap / Nymph: juices from acacia and eucalyptus roots

HABITAT Where this species can find their host plants

RANGE Southeast coast of Australia

THE CICADA KILLER WASP (*Exeirus lateritius*) flies up to a green grocer or another type of cicada, attacks it, and then **DRAGS IT TO ITS UNDERGROUND CATACOMBS.** There, the wasp **LAYS AN EGG ON THE CICADA** so that its larva will have fresh food to feed on.

PERIODICAL CICADA
FAMILY CICADIDAE

Periodical cicadas are among the longest-lived insects in North America. The nymphs live underground sucking juices from tree roots for either 13 or 17 years, depending on the species. When they are ready, they tunnel to the surface, emerging all together, in spectacular numbers. Then they climb up trees or any vertical surface, and molt to become winged adults. They slide out of their old exoskeleton in the evening and spend the night filling out their new wings and hardening their new exoskeleton.

The males sing in large groups to attract females. Each of the species has its own call and some are extremely loud. A male will switch to a unique courtship song when he approaches a female. The two will mate if the female responds favorably to his song. Then the female cuts slits in tree branches and lays her eggs inside. When the little nymphs hatch out, they fall to the ground and burrow down to the tree roots, not to be seen again for many years.

FACTS

COMMON NAME Periodical cicada

SCIENTIFIC NAME *Magicicada* (7 species) / Family: Cicadidae

SIZE *M. septendecim* is up to 1.5 inches (38 mm)

WINGS Yes

FOOD Adult: plant sap / Nymph: juices from tree roots

HABITAT Forests; older neighborhoods with large, old trees

RANGE Eastern United States

HEMIPTERA CICADAS

That's Fact-tastic!

Periodical cicadas are VERY NUTRITIOUS. They are HIGH IN PROTEIN AND LOW IN FAT. On years with a huge bonanza of periodical cicadas, dogs and cats often EAT SO MANY, THEY GET SICK. Many wild animals eat them too—as do people! Have you ever HEARD OF A CICADA PIZZA?

CICADAS GALLERY

There are more than 3,000 species of cicadas around the world. These bugs range in size from 0.8 to two inches (20–50 mm). They often have transparent, or see-through, wings with veins, as well as large eyes.

Members of a cicada population typically hatch from their eggs at the same time. After becoming adults, thousands of cicadas can be seen feeding on tree sap. This behavior often gets cicadas mistaken for locusts, a type of short-horned grasshopper with a tendency to travel in swarms. However, cicadas are more closely related to spittlebugs and leafhoppers (see pages 138–139 and 280).

You'll learn more about cicadas on these pages.

Like all insects, cicadas have six jointed legs. The joints are softer than the insect's exoskeleton—and bendable. This makes movement easier.

This dog-day cicada recently finished molting (shedding) its nymphal exoskeleton. As cicada nymphs grow, they molt several times.

Cicadas have water-repellent wings, which also makes them self-cleaning. When dew forms on the wings, the drops slide off, taking with them any unwanted particles, such as pollen.

A cicada's tubelike mouthpart, which is tucked beneath its head, is its proboscis. Cicadas like those of the *Tibicen* genus, shown here, use these mouthparts to pierce and feed on plants.

A cicada has three small eyes, called ocelli, located between two larger compound eyes. The ocelli help the cicada detect changes in light.

After cicadas molt, they leave behind shell-like "skins." These exoskeletons, discovered alongside a tree trunk, belonged to 17-year cicadas.

A bedbug feeding on a person's arm. Its reddish abdomen is full of its blood meal.

Scanning electron microscope photo of a bedbug

BEDBUG
FAMILY CIMICIDAE

Bedbugs are parasites found throughout the world. They rely on stealth to snatch a blood meal from a human host. By day they hide out in snug places like along mattress edges, but at night, when their human host is asleep, they venture out.

The bugs are attracted to the host's exhaled carbon dioxide and body heat. A hungry bedbug has a flattened abdomen that fills out like a blimp as it feeds. People don't feel when bedbugs feed, but a rash can develop—similar to mosquito bites. Bedbugs can't fly, but they easily hitch a ride to new locations in luggage, on pets, and on clothing.

If a human host isn't available and conditions are right, bedbug larvae can wait a long time for their next blood meal—up to a few months. The adults can wait even longer—up to a year or so!

FACTS

COMMON NAME Bedbug

SCIENTIFIC NAME *Cimex lectularius* / Family: Cimicidae

SIZE 0.16–0.2 inch (4–5 mm)

WINGS Yes: tiny, useless forewings; no hind wings

FOOD Adult and nymph: blood meals

HABITAT Snug hiding places in human habitations

RANGE Worldwide

Specially trained detection **DOGS ARE OFTEN USED TO SNIFF OUT BEDBUGS** in places where they have become pests—mainly in hotels, apartment buildings, and schools.

PEANUT BUG
FAMILY FULGORIDAE

The peanut bug gets its name from the shape of its head. From afar, it looks like an unshelled peanut. But on closer inspection it looks a lot like the head of a cartoon alligator with a toothy grin! The peanut bug sits on tree trunks and branches and drinks sap with its long needlelike proboscis.

The most well known of three peanut bug species is found in Central and South America. Like all peanut bugs, this species is visible on tree trunks, but it has several ways of defending itself from predators. Its mottled color makes it camouflaged from a distance. When disturbed, the peanut bug flashes large eye-spots on its hind wings, giving the appearance of something large and scary. And if that doesn't work, it sprays a substance with a foul odor. Its head might also frighten some predators.

FACTS

OTHER COMMON NAMES Peanut head, peanut head bug, machaca, alligator bug

SCIENTIFIC NAME *Fulgora laternaria* / Family: Fulgoridae

SIZE About 3 inches (76 mm)

WINGS Yes

FOOD Adult and nymph: tree sap

HABITAT Forests

RANGE Central and South America

The "peanut head" is **ACTUALLY A LONG, HOLLOW BULGE AT THE END OF THE BUG'S HEAD** (like an inflated balloon). The bug's eyes are right behind the hollow structure.

That's
Fact-tastic!

Some treehoppers
LIVE IN GROUPS WITH
THE MOTHER watching over her
nymphs. If a small predator pesters
the nymphs, they VIBRATE TO CALL
THEIR MOM. SHE COMES TO THEIR
RESCUE AND CONFRONTS THE
PREDATOR, vibrating her wings and
kicking it off the plant with her
specialized hind legs.

TREE-HOPPER

FAMILIES AETALIONIDAE, MELIZODERIDAE, AND MEMBRACIDAE

Treehoppers win the prize for the most imaginative variety of bug body shapes. They can resemble leaves, thorns, ants, and even helicopters. There are some 3,500 species. Many have a pronotum—a part of the thorax—that is extended to form a hood, horn, or other elaborate sculpture over its body. Treehoppers can be easy to find on small branches, where they pierce the stem to drink sap, although some are well camouflaged.

They communicate with others of their species by vibrating. The vibrations travel through their host plant and are picked up by their neighbors. These sounds can communicate alarm, discovery, or courtship.

Treehoppers drink a lot of plant sap and expel the excess as sugary droplets called honeydew. In a mutualistic relationship, ants drink the sweet honeydew secretions, and, in turn, protect the tree-hoppers from predators.

FACTS

COMMON NAME Treehopper

SCIENTIFIC NAME Families: Aetalionidae, Melizoderidae, and Membracidae

SIZE 0.08–1.2 inches (2–30 mm)

WINGS Yes

FOOD Adult and nymph: plant sap

HABITAT Plant stems

RANGE All regions of the world except New Zealand, Madagascar, and Antarctica

The **SHAPE OF THE PRONOTUM** of this treehopper species, *Bocydium globlare*, **IS HIGHLY UNUSUAL.** Scientists aren't sure if its pronotum serves a purpose.

THORN BUG
FAMILY MEMBRACIDAE

Thorn bugs are a specific type of tree hopper that sit on branches and fool predators by resembling sharp thorns. They feed by inserting their pointy, tubelike mouthparts into a woody branch and sucking up the sap. They are considered pests when large numbers of them feed on and damage ornamental and fruit trees.

A female thorn bug lays about 100 eggs in two rows on a branch. She typically sits over the eggs like a mother hen. Shortly before the eggs hatch, she makes "feeding holes" on the branch for her young. After hatching, the nymphs crowd together and are protected by their watchful mother. Sometimes the siblings push and shove each other to get a prime spot near their mother or in the center of the group where they are safer from predators. The mother only has one brood and lives for about six weeks as an adult—long enough to raise and care for her growing family.

FACTS

COMMON NAME Thorn bug

SCIENTIFIC NAME *Umbonia crassicornis* / Family: Membracidae

SIZE About 0.39 inch (10 mm)

WINGS Yes

FOOD Adult and nymph: plant sap

HABITAT A variety of tropical and subtropical tree and shrub branches

RANGE South America to Mexico, and southern Florida, U.S.A.

A female thorn bug tends her brood. If a wasp or other predator approaches, the nymphs make a vibrating noise—all at the same time—to warn their mother. In response, the **MOTHER APPROACHES THE PREDATOR WHILE FANNING HER WINGS, AND GIVES IT A SWIFT KICK** with her hind legs.

TREEHOPPERS GALLERY

Having strong legs and wings, treehoppers can both jump and fly. They can be extremely small—less than a tenth of an inch up to just over an inch (2–30 mm) long. But if you look at them very closely, you can see the tremendous diversity of forms they take. With about 3,500 species in over 600 genera (plural of genus), the pronotum arising from the upper thorax takes on many surprising shapes that can resemble helmets, swords, thorns, horns, ants, wasps, capes, and more.

Many new species are being discovered, especially in the rainforest canopy. On these pages you can see a small example of treehopper diversity.

This *Stylocentrus* treehopper from South America is feeding on sap with its proboscis (brownish appendage) inserted in a plant stem. It converts the sap into a sweet honeydew favored by ants.

This treehopper (*Heteronotus* sp.) is an ant mimic. Its pronotum extends all the way back over its body.

An adult black-and-white treehopper from South America has a shape similar to other members of its genus.

The pronotum of this *Cladonota* sp. tree-hopper gives the insect a C-shape.

This is a frontal view of a buffalo treehopper.

An adult female and nymphs of the oak treehopper feed on an American chestnut branch.

COCHINEAL SCALE INSECT

FAMILY DACTYLOPIIDAE

Some scale insects look like their name suggests—like little flattened scales. Many are covered in white wax secreted from their bodies.

When a scale insect hatches from its egg, the emerging nymph is called a crawler. In some species, females lose their legs after the first molt and become permanently attached to their host plant. Males keep their legs, and depending on the species, they may or may not have wings as adults. As adults, they only live a day or two, during which they search for females in order to mate.

Although some scale insects are considered pests and harm crops, the cochineal species is valued. Cochineal scale insects cluster together and drink sap from prickly pear cactus pads. Their particular diet allows them to produce a red pigment that can be turned into a dye called carmine. Carmine from cochineal scale insects traditionally has been used for coloring food, fabrics, and cosmetics for centuries.

FACTS

COMMON NAME Cochineal scale insect

SCIENTIFIC NAME *Dactylopius coccus* / Family: Dactylopiidae

SIZE About 0.2 inch (5 mm)

WINGS Male: one pair / Female: no

FOOD Adult and nymph: prickly pear cactus (*Opuntia*)

HABITAT Arid deserts

RANGE Central and South America, desert areas of U.S. and Mexico, and introduced to Australia

A cluster of **LARGE FEMALE COCHINEAL SCALES** attached to a cactus pad

White waxy patches on prickly pear cactus pads are a giveaway that cochineal scale insects live here.

That's
Fact-tastic!

In the late 1700s, a ship captain brought INFECTED PRICKLY PEAR CACTI FROM BRAZIL TO AUSTRALIA in order to start a cochineal dye industry. However, the scale insects died out, and the prickly pear cactus spread to cover some 100,000 square miles (259,000 sq km) in eastern Australia. In the 1920s, a CACTUS-FEEDING MOTH WAS INTRODUCED to control the runaway cactus population.

HIBISCUS HARLEQUIN BUG

FAMILY SCUTELLERIDAE

The hibiscus harlequin bug is a type of jewel bug—a group of shield-shaped insects known for their bright, metallic colors. The male (left) is iridescent blue and red; the female, bright orange with sparkly blue markings. These markings may serve to warn that they are toxic and therefore unsafe to eat.

The bug's colors also help the insect protect its young. After the female hibiscus harlequin lays her eggs, she perches on them. Her bright shield is clearly visible to wasps and other predators that would attack her eggs if they were unattended.

The female hibiscus harlequin continues to tend her brood after they hatch. She keeps an eye on the nymphs as they scoot from one plant to another to feed. Only when the nymphs are capable of taking care of themselves does the mother leave.

FACTS

OTHER COMMON NAME Cotton harlequin bug

SCIENTIFIC NAME Family: Scutelleridae

SIZE Up to 0.8 inch (20 mm)

WINGS Yes

FOOD Adult and nymph: plant juices

HABITAT Wide-ranging (cities, farms, and coastal areas)

RANGE Parts of Australia, New Guinea, and some Pacific islands

Jewel bugs feed on plants the way spiders feed on insects. They **INJECT SALIVA WITH DIGESTIVE ENZYMES INTO A PLANT** and then suck up the juices.

JEWEL BUGS
GALLERY

Jewel bugs are true bugs in the family Scutelleridae. They lay their eggs in clusters on plants. After the embryos inside the eggs mature, they wiggle around until eventually they push their way out through the top of the egg. They emerge as nymphs, then often remain together in their cluster, spending much of their time feeding on plants. Some experts believe that this clustering behavior makes the group look larger—and more intimidating to predators.

Jewel bugs typically have bright iridescent colors, such as green, red, purple, pink, and blue. Their iridescence is not caused by pigments, but by how light interacts with the surface of their bodies.

The shiny creatures shown here are just some of the amazing jewel bugs found around the world. Check them out!

Color and pattern not only vary among different species of jewel bugs, but they also change as a jewel bug develops.

This bug's membranous hind wings are folded up under its leathery forewings.

Although most jewel bugs are harmless to plants, some species have been known to cause great damage to crops.

The jewel bug's shield is called a scutellum. It's formed by the last section of the insect's thorax and extends down to cover the abdomen. This makes jewel bugs different from beetles, whose cover is formed by hardened forewings.

Like a stink bug (see pages 128–129), a jewel bug can release foul-smelling chemicals from the sides of its thorax when threatened.

While feeding, jewel bugs inject enzymes from their saliva into the plant. This helps liquefy the plant so that the jewel bug can drink it up.

STINK BUG

FAMILY PENTATOMIDAE

Get a whiff of this: **When stink bugs feel** threatened by a predator, they let out a nasty, foul-smelling liquid. The odor is so bad, it's often enough to drive some predators away. It's no wonder why these critters are named as they are. The stink bug's smelly liquid is a mixture of compounds that are produced by glands located in the insect's body. In the adult bug, the glands are found in its thorax, while nymphs possess the glands in their abdomen.

Stink bugs don't just pose a problem to predators; they can also be a nuisance to people. Each year, these bugs cause many millions of dollars worth of damage to crops. They also get into people's homes. And if you think that we are immune to the bug's stinkiness, think again. Many people who accidentally step on the bug smell a skunk-like odor. *Ew.*

FACTS

COMMON NAME Stink bug

SCIENTIFIC NAME Family: Pentatomidae

SIZE About 0.2–0.75 inch (5–19 mm)

WINGS Yes

FOOD Adult and nymph: mainly plant sap; some species eat insects

HABITAT Gardens and farms

RANGE Worldwide except Antarctica

This wheel bug nymph—a type of assassin bug—plunges its beak into a treehopper.

ASSASSIN BUG

FAMILY REDUVIIDAE

Unlike many bugs, which only kill prey that wander into their immediate territory, assassin bugs actively seek out their victims. How do they do it? That depends on the type of assassin bug.

The thread-legged assassin bug (subfamily Emesinae) preys on web-building spiders. When it comes across a web, it plucks the threads. This mimics the movement of prey caught in the web. The spider, thinking it has caught a meal, scurries over—and ends up becoming a meal itself!

One assassin bug (*Ptilocerus ochraceus*) has tufts of red hair on its abdomen, which attract ants. These tufts of hair secrete a poisonous fluid. When the ants lick the fluid, they become paralyzed—an easy lunch for the bug.

Millipede assassin bugs prefer to hunt in groups. They team up to take down millipedes that are often 10 times their size!

FACTS

COMMON NAME Assassin bug

SCIENTIFIC NAME Family: Reduviidae

SIZE Some species can grow more than 1 inch (25 mm)

WINGS Yes

FOOD Adult: insects / Nymph: dead insects and sometimes other members of its species

HABITAT Most often on shrubs and dense vegetation

RANGE Worldwide

An ant-eating assassin bug, *Acanthaspis petax*, **PILES THE CORPSES OF ITS VICTIMS ONTO ITS BODY.** This makes it look a lot larger than it is, and thus **INTIMIDATES SOME WOULD-BE PREDATORS.**

GIANT WATER BUG

FAMILY BELOSTOMATIDAE

As its name suggests, the giant water bug is one big bug. Some species can grow to be more than four inches (100 mm) long. That's longer than the width of an average human hand!

The bugs have a hefty appetite to match their large size. One species, *Kirkaldyia deyrolli,* has been seen eating a pond turtle in Japan!

A giant water bug relies on its powerful forelegs to snag its prey. It then uses its sharp beak to pierce the victim's body and inject it with a powerful toxin that breaks down tissue. Once the prey's tissue has been liquefied, the giant water bug can begin to feed.

FACTS

OTHER COMMON NAMES Toe-biter, electric-light bug

SCIENTIFIC NAME Family: Belostomatidae

SIZE More than 4 inches (100 mm)

WINGS Yes

FOOD Adult: bugs, small fish, frogs, and salamanders / Nymph: small aquatic invertebrates

HABITAT Clear, freshwater streams and ponds

RANGE Worldwide, but most diverse in tropics

The females of certain giant water bugs **GLUE THEIR EGGS ON THE BACKS OF MALES.** The males then guard the eggs until they hatch.

The giant water bug uses its
flat, oarlike hind legs to help
propel itself through water.

These two water striders create dimples on the water's surface, but stay above water. Even rain and waves can't drown them.

WATER STRIDER
FAMILY GERRIDAE

Water striders skip easily across the water's surface. Thousands of minuscule hairs on their bodies hold air and repel water, making it easy to stay afloat. Their long, slender legs distribute their weight over a large surface area as they take advantage of the high surface tension of the water.

Each of their three pairs of legs has a different function. The short front pair have tiny claws and are used to grasp and hold prey. The middle legs act as paddles to propel the body across the water's surface, while the back legs help steer.

Most live in freshwater habitats like rivers, streams, and lakes. However, about 10 percent of the species, called sea skaters, actually live offshore on the surface of the ocean and are the only insects to live in that habitat!

Water striders are predators that feed by piercing their prey and sucking out the juices. They can detect when an insect or spider falls into the water by the ripples they create on the water's surface.

FACTS

OTHER COMMON NAMES Water skeeters, water scooters, water bugs, pond skaters

SCIENTIFIC NAME Family: Gerridae (more than 1,700 named species)

SIZE 0.08–1.42 inches (2–36 mm)

WINGS Depends on the species

FOOD Mostly floating insects and spiders, also plankton

HABITAT On the surface of fresh water or salt water

RANGE Worldwide except New Zealand and Antarctica

Water striders **CONSUME PREY ON THE SURFACE OF THE WATER.** This young water strider has caught and pierced a fly, and is **SUCKING UP ITS INSIDES.**

EGGPLANT LACE BUG

FAMILY TINGIDAE

Eggplant lace bugs look nothing like eggplants. Instead, they have striking wings and a pronotum (part of the thorax) that resemble lace. The bug got the name "eggplant" in 1913, after it harmed many eggplant crops in Virginia, U.S.A.

The bugs may have a bad reputation where crops are concerned, but they have a good reputation as parents. The female eggplant lace bug is especially attentive. She guards her clutch of eggs closely, leaving only for brief periods to feed. After her nymphs break free from their eggs, she continues to care for them. Sometimes, she'll lead them from one leaf to another to feed. During this migration, she scoots from the front of the group to the back, making sure that all the nymphs are together and heading in the right direction. If she spots a straggler, she gently nudges it back into the group with her antennae.

FACTS

COMMON NAME Eggplant lace bug

SCIENTIFIC NAME *Gargaphia solani* / Family: Tingidae

SIZE 0.16 inch (4 mm)

WINGS Yes

FOOD Adult and nymph: liquids sucked from tomatoes, potatoes, and eggplants

HABITAT Various crops including tomatoes, potatoes, eggplant

RANGE Parts of the United States

Lace bugs are plant feeders, and can spend their entire lives on the same plant. They prefer to hang out on the underside of leaves, where they suck up sap from the plant's tissue.

That's Fact-tastic!

Mother eggplant lace bugs **KEEP A CLOSE WATCH OVER THEIR NYMPHS,** which are vulnerable to attack. If a predator approaches, **THE MOTHERS FAN THEIR WINGS AND RUSH** toward the predator to scare it off.

137

SPITTLE-BUG

SUPERFAMILY CERCOPOIDEA

Don't be grossed out if you see a ball of foamy "spit" coating the stalk of a plant. A young spittlebug may be nestled inside!

After spittlebug nymphs hatch from their eggs, they feed on plant sap. The nymphs take in more sap than they need for food. The extra sap gets mixed with air and urine and comes out of its abdomen as a bubbly mass. This foam becomes a home to the nymph until it transforms into an adult. The foam keeps the nymph's body moist and helps conceal the young bug from predators.

FACTS

OTHER COMMON NAME Froghopper

SCIENTIFIC NAME Superfamily: Cercopoidea

SIZE 0.12–1.06 inches (3–27 mm)

WINGS Yes

FOOD Adult and nymph: sap from grasses and other herbs

HABITAT Mainly grasslands and garden plants

RANGE Worldwide

Adult spittlebugs are known as froghoppers because of their **INCREDIBLE JUMPING SKILLS.** Most frog-hoppers can leap more than two feet (60 cm) into the air. That's as much as **100 TIMES THEIR BODY LENGTH.**

APHID

FAMILY APHIDIDAE

When it comes to surviving in the wild, it's who you know that counts. Few insects know this better than the aphid.

Aphids are tiny plant-feeding insects that rarely measure more than 0.4 inch (10 mm) long. Their small size can make them vulnerable to predators, which is why some species rely on the help of others to get by.

One North American species, *Pemphigus obesinymphae,* raises an army of daughters that defend the colony. If a predator, such as a lacewing larva, threatens the colony, the soldier daughters swarm over it. They pierce the predator with their sharp mouthparts, harming and sometimes killing it.

Other species, such as the woolly alder aphid *(Prociphilus tessellatus)* rely on the help of ants to ward off their attackers. Do the ants get anything in return for their bodyguard duties? Yes! The aphids excrete a sugary liquid called honeydew that the ants feed on.

FACTS

OTHER COMMON NAMES Greenbug, greenfly, plant louse

SCIENTIFIC NAME Family: Aphididae

SIZE 0.04–0.4 inch (1–10 mm)

WINGS Winged and wingless forms are found in many species

FOOD Adult and nymph: plant sap of particular plants

HABITAT Trees, shrubs, and garden plants

RANGE Worldwide, but occur most often in temperate zones

Aphids are **SOMETIMES CALLED "ANT COWS"** because their relationship to ants is similar to that of cattle to humans. **ANTS TEND THEIR APHIDS AND FEED ON THEIR HONEYDEW** just as humans tend cattle and feed on their milk!

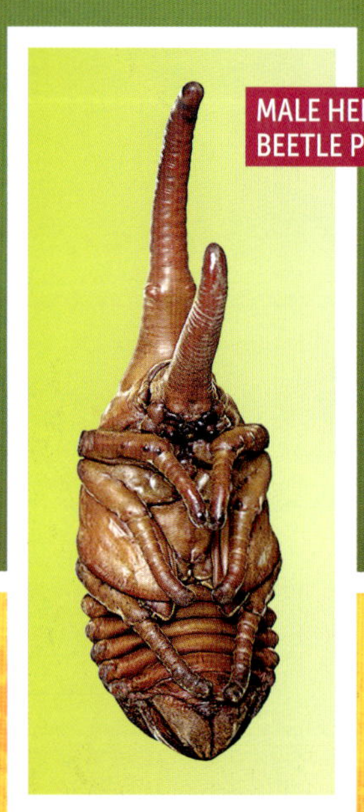

MALE HERCULES BEETLE PUPA

MOSQUITO LARVAE AND PUPAE UNDERWATER. THE PUPAE HAVE THE BIG HEADS.

THE LARVA OF A *DYSPHANIA MILITARIS* MOTH CRAWLING ON A BRANCH

MONARCH PUPA

CLOSE-UP OF A LADYBUG LARVA

CHAPTER THREE

COMPLETE
METAMORPHOSIS

INSECT ORDERS

Young insects, called larvae, undergo complete metamorphosis, which means they change dramatically as they develop and grow. A wriggling larva hardly looks like the winged adult that it will become. Not until it is almost ready to emerge from its pupa do its wings become visible.

Here you'll find a list of all the different orders of insects with complete metamorphosis. The scientific name for the order is noted below the common name. The figures below it are estimates of the number of insects in that order that have already been named and described. That number is constantly changing. Many additional insect specimens are in museum collections around the world waiting to be described, and many more have yet to be collected. Also, scientists sometimes change the name of an order to reflect new information they discover about the insects within it. To find out about the different species within an order, just turn to the pages noted.

BEETLES
Coleoptera
coh · lee · OP · ter · uh
About 400,000 species
pages 146–179

DOBSONFLIES
Megaloptera
meg · uh · LOP · ter · uh
About 300 species
pages 180–181

ANTLIONS AND LACEWINGS
Neuroptera
NUR · OP · ter · uh
About 6,000 species
pages 182–185

SNAKEFLIES
Raphidioptera
ruh · fid · ee · OP · ter · uh
About 250 species
pages 186–187

WASPS, BEES, AND ANTS
Hymenoptera
high · men · OP · ter · uh
About 130,000 species
pages 188–215

FLEAS
Siphonaptera
sigh · fun · APP · ter · uh
About 2,600 species
pages 216–217

HANGINGFLIES
Mecoptera
meh · COP · ter · uh
About 600 species
pages 218–219

TWISTED-WING PARASITES
Strepsiptera
strep · SIP · ter · uh
About 600 species
pages 220–221

FLIES
Diptera
DIP · ter · uh
About 150,000 species
pages 222–233

CADDISFLIES
Trichoptera
tri · COP · ter · uh
About 16,000 species
pages 234–235

BUTTERFLIES AND MOTHS
Lepidoptera
leh · pih · DOP · ter · uh
About 175,000 species
pages 236–269

RHINOCEROS BEETLE

LADYBUG
FAMILY COCCINELLIDAE

Don't be misled by the common name "ladybug." Ladybugs are not true bugs (Hemiptera) but are instead beetles. There are more than 6,000 species in the family, all with dome-shaped bodies. Both adults and larvae are voracious predators, eating many aphids and scale insects (see pages 140–141 and 122–123) found on plants. During the winter, they hibernate on the warmer south side of trees and buildings and in rotting logs and leaf litter. If they can, they go indoors.

As predators, ladybugs control populations of aphids and scale insects that may damage gardens and crops. They in turn have their own predators, like birds, spiders, and some insects. But they have a few defenses against them: Ladybugs taste bad, they can release a foul odor, and they can play dead.

Their average life span is about a year.

That's
Fact-tastic!
Ladybugs are
NOT JUST FEMALE,
despite their name, and YOU
CAN'T TELL THEIR AGE BY THE
NUMBER OF SPOTS on their backs,
which is a common myth. But the
number of spots does help
to identify the species
of ladybug.

GOLDEN TORTOISE BEETLE

FAMILY CHRYSOMELIDAE

Tortoise beetles look like they have an upside-down bowl over their backs, legs, and head. The bowl is actually their front wings and part of their thorax. It protects them so that predators, like ants, can't grab hold of them.

The golden tortoise beetle is named for its golden, jewel-like appearance on morning glory leaves, their preferred food. However, the bug isn't always golden. It can change its colors. The color change depends on the amount of fluids between layers inside their wings. The fluid is controlled by microscopic valves.

This color change once fooled scientists into believing that they were observing different species of beetles, not one. They even gave the beetle different names.

FACTS

OTHER COMMON NAME Sweet potato leaf beetle

SCIENTIFIC NAME *Charidotella sexpunctata* / Family: Chrysomelidae

SIZE 0.2–0.28 inch (5–7 mm)

WINGS Yes (their forewings are hardened wing covers and their hind wings are for flying)

FOOD Adult and larva: morning glories

HABITAT Found on morning glories

RANGE North America

The larva of the golden tortoise beetle has an effective way of defending itself. It has a long, **FORKLIKE EXTENSION** at the end of its abdomen that **HOLDS LARGE GOBS OF FECES.** When it holds this extension (called a **FECAL PARASOL**) over its body, predators ignore it.

TORTOISE BEETLES
GALLERY

Tortoise beetles range in size from 0.2 to 0.4 inch (5–10 mm) long. In addition to morning glory leaves, they like to eat the leaves of sweet potato, bindweed, and other plants in the same family.

There are more than 3,000 species of tortoise beetles. They live all over the world. Many come in bright, shimmery colors such as gold, red, and green. Some colors are caused by pigmented liquids inside the outer part of the insect's body. These liquids can also help change a tortoise beetle's colors. Some species can change their color in response to predator attacks or other external threats.

In addition to their protective shells, some tortoise beetles are known for their great parenting skills. After laying their eggs, most female tortoise beetles watch over their brood to protect them from predators. The adult beetles may even remain with their young after they hatch.

Here are six more species of tortoise beetles for you to discover.

Many tortoise beetles have jewel-like shells, as shown here. The shell covers all parts of the beetle, except for its antennae.

This tortoise beetle lifts its hardened elytra (forewings) and spreads its hind wings in order to fly.

This female tortoise beetle closely guards her tightly packed eggs. She will protect them from predators such as ants and wasps.

Tortoise beetles typically hatch, feed, and mate on the same plant.

Like other tortoise beetles, the target tortoise beetle from the Amazon rainforest can clamp itself tightly to a leaf for protection.

This tortoise beetle looks like a crab from this angle. Its head and antennae are clearly visible. Like all insects, tortoise beetles use their antennae to help sense their environment.

VIOLIN BEETLE

FAMILY CARABIDAE

Violin beetles live upside down on the underside of shelf fungi and under tree bark in the tropical rainforests of Southeast Asia. They get their name from the violin-like shape of their body. Their flattened shape allows them to hunt invertebrates in cramped spaces. Having long legs lets them chase down their prey quickly.

A rounded notch on their elytra (front wings) provides an opening for them to extend a pair of turrets (projections) on their abdomen. They can aim the turrets toward an enemy and squirt it with a painful acid. The acid is known to be so strong that it can paralyze a person's hand for a day or more.

Violin beetles dig a chamber in shelf fungi to lay their eggs and provide a home for their larvae as they grow up.

The violin beetle is in the huge family of "ground beetles." It's one of more than 40,000 known species. Although the family is known as ground beetles, many are found in tree canopies, especially in the rainforest.

FACTS

COMMON NAME Violin beetle

SCIENTIFIC NAME *Mormolyce* / Family: Carabidae

SIZE 2.4–4 inches (60–100 mm)

WINGS Yes (their forewings are hardened wing covers and their hind wings are for flying)

FOOD Adult: invertebrates such as insect larvae and snails / Larva: small invertebrates

HABITAT Under bark, and in bracket fungi

RANGE Southeast Asia

COLEOPTERA BEETLES

That's Fact-tastic!
The violin beetle has been DEPICTED ON POSTAGE STAMPS in several countries, demonstrating pride in this iconic insect.

Some bombardier beetle species are **ABLE TO FLY.** But before the beetle can take off, it **MUST OPEN ITS WING CASINGS** and then unfurl its wings. This can take a bit of time, which is a problem when a predator is quickly approaching. Fortunately, the beetle's **SPRAY MECHANISM CAN BE QUICKLY DEPLOYED,** giving the beetle the time it needs to set up and make its getaway.

BOMBARDIER BEETLE

FAMILY CARABIDAE

There are nearly 40,000 species in this huge family, and more than 500 of them are known as bombardier beetles. When an animal or person disturbs them, they take aim and shoot out a boiling-hot, skin-blistering liquid!

The liquid is formed from a mix of chemical compounds in a pair of reservoirs in the beetle's abdomen. The beetle can force the chemicals into a reaction chamber at the tip of its abdomen when it's alarmed. There the chemicals react with enzymes to make the boiling liquid.

When the beetle feels threatened, it swivels its abdomen in the direction of its target and shoots the hot liquid. The beetle can aim forward and backward, and side to side, so there is no escape for its attacker.

If a toad tosses a bombardier beetle in its mouth and swallows it, the toad will vomit the beetle up and both the beetle and the toad will live. But if another insect gets blasted, it won't survive.

FACTS

COMMON NAME Bombardier beetle

SCIENTIFIC NAME Family: Carabidae

SIZE Mostly under 1 inch (25 mm)

WINGS Yes (their forewings are hardened wing covers and their hind wings are for flying)

FOOD Adult and larva: small insects

HABITAT Mostly temperate woodlands and grasslands

RANGE Worldwide except Antarctica

FIREFLY
FAMILY LAMPYRIDAE

Fireflies are beetles, not flies. Like stars twinkling on a summer night, fireflies catch our attention and imagination. More important, they draw the attention of their potential mates with their flashing signals. There are some 2,000 species in the firefly family, each with its own blinking patterns. Some types gather together in large numbers and blink on and off in perfect unison!

How do they make light? Fireflies use special cells inside light organs in their abdomen. Oxygen combines with a chemical called luciferin in the cells. Together with an enzyme they make light. The chemical reaction is known as bioluminescence.

Adult fireflies lay their eggs on the ground. Both larvae and pupae light up, but they don't blink like adults. The larvae might live a couple of years underground, but the adults die after a few weeks.

FACTS

OTHER COMMON NAME Lightning bug

SCIENTIFIC NAME Family: Lampyridae

SIZE Up to 1 inch (25 mm)

WINGS Yes in most

FOOD Adult: some feed on pollen and mites; others don't eat at all / Larva: small invertebrates

HABITAT Humid areas

RANGE Temperate and tropical regions worldwide

Scientists have **TRANSFERRED THE "LIGHT" GENE** found in fireflies into **OTHER ORGANISMS,** including mice, monkeys, cats, and tobacco plants.

Fireflies all
lit up, flying
over a field

PIGGYBACK BEETLE
FAMILY HISTERIDAE

Is that an ant or a beetle in the photo on the right? It's both!

In a tropical rainforest in the middle of Costa Rica, a bizarre little beetle comes out at night and hitchhikes a ride on the back of an army ant worker. It uses its long mandibles like a pair of pliers to latch onto the ant's slender midsection. Its body mimics the ant's abdomen, making the ant look like it has two abdomens—not that looks matter in the dark. The beetle rides by night on its host as the colony of army ants hunt for prey. By hitchhiking, perhaps the beetle can find new sources of food. The beetle also mimics the smell of the ants. This might be the reason the ants don't attack it. A lot more needs to be learned about this species of beetle, which was named in 2017.

The beetle belongs to a family of around 3,900 species of predators that are called clown beetles or hister beetles.

FACTS

COMMON NAME Piggyback beetle

SCIENTIFIC NAME *Nymphister kronaueri* / Family: Histeridae

SIZE 0.055–0.063 inch (1.4–1.6 mm)

WINGS Yes

FOOD Unknown, probably ant larvae or ant prey

HABITAT Where army ants *(Eciton mexicanum)* are found

RANGE Known only in the rainforest at La Selva Biological Station in Costa Rica, but probably more widespread

Insect collections have specimens that are **PINNED INSIDE DISPLAY CASES ALONG WITH IMPORTANT INFORMATION.** If the insect is very tiny (like the piggyback beetle) it is first glued to a paper tab, then the tab is pinned down.

That's
Fact-tastic!

The round, reddish brown beetle on the right is **ATTACHED BY ITS JAWS TO AN ANT.** The ant's real abdomen is the yellow-brown part.

Goliath beetles are named after the **BIBLICAL CHARACTER GOLIATH.** In this famous tale, Goliath is **A MENACING GIANT** who stands more than nine feet (2.7 m) tall.

GOLIATH BEETLE
FAMILY SCARABAEIDAE

The Goliath is one of the world's largest beetles. It's also the heaviest. This colossal insect can measure up to 4.3 inches (110 mm) long and weigh up to 2.1 ounces (60 g). A Goliath beetle larva weighs up to 3.5 ounces (100 g). That makes it as heavy as some cell phones!

How does the Goliath beetle get so big? As a larva, the beetle feeds on plenty of high-protein foods. It continues to feed as it develops.

When the larva finally stops growing, it burrows into the ground, where it enters its pupal stage. During this stage, its tissues break down and are reorganized into an adult form. Because of the Goliath beetle's large size, this can take several months. When the process is complete, an adult Goliath beetle emerges.

FACTS

COMMON NAME Goliath beetle

SCIENTIFIC NAME *Goliathus goliatus* / Family: Scarabaeidae

SIZE 2–4.3 inches (50–110 mm)

WINGS Yes (their forewings are hardened wing covers and their hind wings are for flying)

FOOD Adult: tree sap and rotting fruit / Larva: plant matter, dung, and animal remains

HABITAT Equatorial forests and savannas

RANGE Equatorial region of Africa

SACRED SCARAB
FAMILY SCARABAEIDAE

Sacred scarab beetles have a gross habit. They roll dung balls. That's not all—they eat them too! The beetles also use the dung balls to house their eggs and feed their young. The female lays a single egg inside a specially sculpted dung ball, which she keeps in an underground chamber. Inside, the larva will feed on the dung and grow.

The sacred scarab got its name because of its history. The ancient Egyptians likened their god of the sunrise to the beetles. They noted the similarity between how the scarab beetle rolled its dung ball to how the sun rolled across the sky each day.

These beetles do a huge service to the environment by eating and burying animal dung, which fertilizes and loosens the soil.

FACTS

COMMON NAME   Sacred scarab

SCIENTIFIC NAME   *Scarabaeus sacer* / Family: Scarabaeidae

SIZE   1.1–1.26 inches (28–32 mm)

WINGS   Yes (their forewings are hardened wing covers and their hind wings are for flying)

FOOD   Adult and larva: animal dung

HABITAT   In coastal dunes and marshes

RANGE   Around the Mediterranean Sea

COLEOPTERA BEETLES

That's
Fact-tastic!

DRIED
DUNG BEETLES are
used for all kinds of
health treatments in
TRADITIONAL CHINESE
MEDICINE.

Hide beetles are **USED BY SCIENTISTS** at natural history museums to **EAT AWAY FUR AND SKIN FROM THE BONES OF DEAD ANIMALS.** This helps the scientists prepare the bones for museum exhibitions.

HIDE BEETLE

FAMILY DERMESTIDAE

Hide beetles, dark and hairy, are best known for their somewhat creepy diet. They feed on dead animals—and that includes humans!

This ability of theirs makes hide beetles somewhat unique. Most insects would be unable to digest an animal's keratin—a protein that makes up skin, fingernails, and hair—because the substance is too tough. But hide beetles have special enzymes in their digestive tract that help break down the material.

The beetle's diet has made it a favorite among forensic scientists. When these crime-scene specialists see the bugs on or near a dead body, they know the victim has been dead for quite some time. That's because the bugs only show up late in the body's decomposition process.

FACTS

COMMON NAME Hide beetle

SCIENTIFIC NAME *Dermestes maculatus* / Family: Dermestidae

SIZE 0.22–0.4 inch (5.5–10 mm)

WINGS Yes (their forewings are hardened wing covers and their hind wings are for flying)

FOOD Adult and larva: dead animals

HABITAT Many different habitats

RANGE Worldwide except Antarctica

This close-up of a hide beetle shows that the insect is **COVERED WITH TINY HAIRS,** which are called setae. The hairs produce a **DISTINCT PATTERN ON EACH SPECIES.** Scientists use these unique patterns to help identify hide beetles in the field.

HEADLIGHT ELATER
FAMILY ELATERIDAE

Shortly after sunset, the large headlight elater beetle becomes active. It gets its name from the two bright light organs on the upper part of its thorax. The headlights, along with a band on the lower part of its body, glow in the dark. In fact, the lights can get so bright, people are known to hold a headlight elater like a flashlight to light the trail in front of them. These beetles don't blink quickly like fireflies do, but they can signal to potential mates by keeping the lights on for a long period of time and blinking occasionally. The eggs, larvae, and pupae also glow.

There are various species of headlight elaters. The species *Pyrophorus noctilucus* is the largest of them. Headlight elaters are a few of the 9,300 or so species of click beetles. Click beetles snap their bodies very forcefully, catapulting themselves into the air about a foot or so high, and they can flip over when they're on their backs. They mainly use their click mechanism to defend themselves from predators.

FACTS

COMMON NAME Headlight elater

SCIENTIFIC NAME *Pyrophorus noctilucus* / Family: Elateridae

SIZE 1.6–2 inches (40–50 mm)

WINGS Yes (their forewings are hardened wing covers and their hind wings are for flying)

FOOD Adult: pollen, fermenting fruit, and small insects / Larva: plant matter and small invertebrates

HABITAT Forests

RANGE Northern half of South America, Panama, Mexico, southern U.S., Hawaii, and Caribbean islands

COLEOPTERA BEETLES

RED MILKWEED BEETLE
FAMILY CERAMBYCIDAE

The best place to find the red milkweed beetle is—you guessed it—on milkweed plants. Milkweeds have toxins that most insects can't handle, but red milkweed beetles have adapted to feeding on these plants without being harmed. In fact, they use the toxins they take in for protection. Predators that munch on the beetle experience a nasty taste surprise—and learn to keep the critter off their lunch menu in the future!

The beetle's milkweed diet isn't its only interesting feature. Unlike most insects, it has four eyes. The base of each antenna is positioned such that one eye lies above it and one below.

These beetles belong to a huge family with about 35,000 species. They are commonly known as longhorn beetles, named for their extremely long antennae.

One species of longhorn beetle (*Cyrtophorus verrucosus*) **IS AN ANT MIMIC FROM NORTH AMERICA.** It not only looks like an ant, it also **BEHAVES LIKE ONE** by waving its antennae and walking in a zigzag motion.

FACTS

OTHER COMMON NAMES Eastern milkweed longhorn, four-eyed beetle

SCIENTIFIC NAME *Tetraopes tetrophthalmus* / Family: Cerambycidae

SIZE 0.4–0.63 inch (10–16 mm)

WINGS Yes (their forewings are hardened wing covers and their hind wings are for flying)

FOOD Adult: foliage and flowers of milkweed / Larva: stems and roots of milkweed

HABITAT Wherever the host plant is present, especially open areas

RANGE Eastern and central North America

GIANT CARRION BEETLE

FAMILY SILPHIDAE

This big scavenger is an environmental hero. It feeds on dead, decaying animals and buries the leftovers in the ground. This helps recycle the dead matter into the ecosystem. The giant carrion beetle not only eats carrion, but raises its young on it too. In fact, these beetles will fight over a carcass—the winning male and female get to bury it!

Unlike most insects, male and female burying beetles raise their larvae together. After the female lays between one and 30 eggs next to the carcass, both mom and dad feed and tend their young. The larvae eat for about a week, then become pupae in the soil.

Unfortunately, giant carrion beetles are critically endangered. They have been drastically decreasing in numbers, and they have disappeared from 90 percent of their historic range. The reason for the decline isn't clear, though some experts believe pesticides and habitat loss could be to blame.

FACTS

OTHER COMMON NAME American burying beetle

SCIENTIFIC NAME *Nicrophorus americanus* / Family: Silphidae

SIZE 1–1.8 inches (25–45 mm)

WINGS Yes (their forewings are hardened wing covers and their hind wings are for flying)

FOOD Adult and larva: carrion

HABITAT Wherever carcasses of birds and small mammals can be found

RANGE Once widespread, now in only a few U.S. states and being reintroduced into others

A giant carrion beetle **PREPARES A DEAD DOVE** for burial.

That's Fact-tastic!

The giant carrion beetle has CHEMICAL RECEPTORS on its clublike antennae that can smell dead animals from ALMOST TWO MILES (3.2 KM) AWAY.

BLUE FUNGUS BEETLE
FAMILY EROTYLIDAE

Not all beetles feed on plants or animals. Some, like the blue fungus beetle, can't produce the enzymes needed to break down plant or animal tissues, so they feed on fungi because it does the job for them.

Fungi, such as mushrooms, are nature's decomposers. They break down and digest nonliving organic matter such as decaying trees and leaves, as well as dead animals. The fungi absorb nutrients from the matter they decompose. So when the blue fungus beetle eats the fungi, it gets the nutrients it needs to survive.

Mother beetles of this species also use the fungus as a shelter for their eggs. When the larvae emerge from their shells, they don't have to go far for food. They are immediately treated to a fungus meal.

FACTS

COMMON NAME Blue fungus beetle

SCIENTIFIC NAME *Cypherotylus californicus* / Family: Erotylidae

SIZE 0.5–0.8 inch (12–20 mm)

WINGS Yes (their forewings are hardened wing covers and their hind wings are for flying)

FOOD Adult and larva: wood-rotting fungi

HABITAT Moist areas at higher elevations

RANGE Southwestern North America and northern Mexico

The blue fungus beetle belongs to the family known as the **"PLEASING FUNGUS BEETLES."** Members of this family are **OFTEN BRIGHTLY COLORED.** They may also have **PATTERNS SUCH AS DOTS, STRIPES, AND ZIGZAGS.**

DARKLING BEETLE

FAMILY TENEBRIONIDAE

There are approximately 20,000 species of darkling beetles in the world. "Darkling" refers to the dark-colored elytra, or hardened fore-wings, sported by many of these creatures.

The name also refers to the insect's nocturnal habits. The beetle is mainly active at night, when it forages for food such as insect larvae and decaying plant and animal matter.

Foraging at night gives the darkling beetle some protection from predators that would have no trouble spotting the critter in daylight. However, if a predator does manage to detect the beetle, the beetle will fight back. Many species of darklings, such as the pinacate beetle, blast predators with a smelly liquid. They are sometimes known as desert stink beetles.

FACTS

COMMON NAME Darkling beetle

SCIENTIFIC NAME Family: Tenebrionidae

SIZE 0.08–2 inches (2–50 mm)

WINGS Yes (their forewings are hardened wing covers and their hind wings are for flying)

FOOD Adult and larva: plant matter, some decomposing animal matter, and fungi

HABITAT Dry and arid regions

RANGE Worldwide

Some darkling beetle species live in deserts, where water isn't always available. To stay hydrated, they **TAKE IN WATER FROM FOG THAT CONDENSES** on their forewings. They position themselves so their **HEADS FACE DOWN** and the **CONDENSED WATER ROLLS INTO THEIR MOUTHS.**

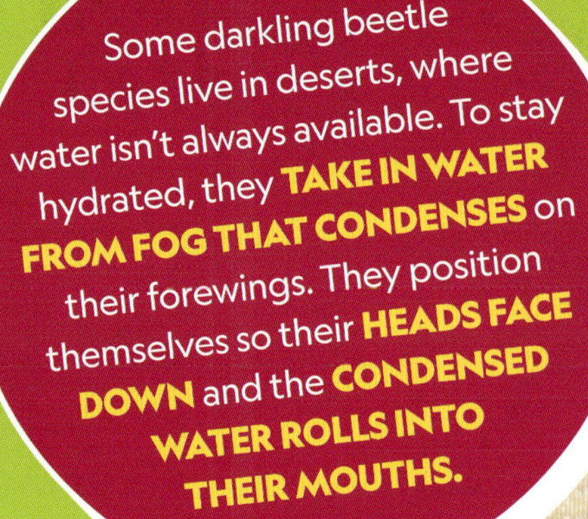

The darkling beetle shown here—a member of the *Alphitobius* genus—is from Tanzania, Africa.

That's
Fact-tastic!
The giraffe
weevil's NECK IS
JOINTED, allowing
it to bend.

GIRAFFE WEEVIL
FAMILY ATTELABIDAE

A **weevil is a type of small beetle that's known** for its noselike snout. Weevils often use their snouts to bore holes into the plants, fruits, or nuts that they feed on. For some weevils, their snout isn't their only striking feature. The male giraffe weevil has a superlong neck that is longer than the insect's body.

Male giraffe weevils use their necks to fight each other for the right to mate with a female. It's not common for males to kill each other during the battle, but the fighting can get pretty fierce. You might say the competition is neck and neck.

Giraffe weevils are especially fond of the small trees in Madagascar that have been named after them. They're called giraffe weevil trees.

FACTS

COMMON NAME Giraffe weevil

SCIENTIFIC NAME *Trachelophorus giraffa /* Family: Attelabidae

SIZE Up to 1 inch (25 mm)

WINGS Yes (their forewings are hardened wing covers and their hind wings are for flying)

FOOD Adult and larva: small tree leaves

HABITAT Forests

RANGE Madagascar

Some weevil species, like the **CHESTNUT WEEVIL** (*Curculio caryatrypes*), don't just **USE THEIR LONG SNOUTS** to feed. They also use them to **DRILL HOLES INTO NUTS,** where they lay their eggs.

WEEVILS GALLERY

Weevils are a type of beetle with some 97,000 known species. Many of them have an elongated head called a snout with mouthparts at the tip. They chew their way into the grains, fruits, and roots of plants. Some weevils do this to extract food or to carve out a home for their eggs. Most weevils start life on the plants that they eat, and some weevils are pests on crop plants.

Although some species, like the giraffe weevil, can be a whole inch long, most weevils are smaller, rarely exceeding a quarter of an inch (6 mm). A weevil's tiny size can make it an easy target for larger predators, like spiders and birds. When most weevils are threatened by a predator, they react by dropping to the ground and playing dead. Since many weevils are similar in color to soil, they go undetected.

Check out the six species on this page.

This palmetto weevil is lifting its elytra and unfolding its hind wings in preparation for flight. Palmetto weevils are known to cause a lot of damage to palm trees.

Many weevils draw up their legs, fall over, and play dead when discovered by a predator.

The color of this flashy blue weevil is the result of light reflecting off tiny scales that cover the insect's body.

A few weevil species, like this one from the Amazon rainforest, have snouts that are longer than their bodies!

This close-up of a weevil shows the many light-sensitive cells that make up the insect's compound eyes.

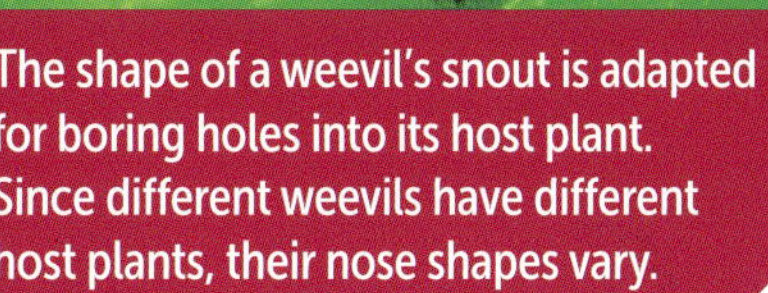

The shape of a weevil's snout is adapted for boring holes into its host plant. Since different weevils have different host plants, their nose shapes vary.

That's
Fact-tastic!

A female eastern dobsonfly
**COVERS HER EGGS WITH A
CLEAR FLUID.** When the fluid
dries, it turns a white color
that **RESEMBLES LARGE BIRD
DROPPINGS.** This helps
CAMOUFLAGE THE EGGS
from predators.

EASTERN DOBSONFLY
FAMILY CORYDALIDAE

The male eastern dobsonfly has long, curved mandibles, or pincers, that measure up to 1.6 inches (40 mm) long. That's about three times the length of his head! His mandibles look like they pack quite a bite, but they're actually harmless.

The male uses his mandibles during courtship and mating. He'll flaunt his jaws in front of a female to impress her, or he'll use them to wrestle other males. The victor of the match wins the right to mate with the female. The female lays her eggs on leaves overhanging a stream. The eggs hatch and the small larvae drop into the water.

The larvae develop gills and are called hellgrammites. They live, often for years, under rocks in streams, rivers, and lakes. The jaws of a dobsonfly larva are much smaller, but not as harmless as the adult's. These maturing dobsonflies use their sharp, forward-pointing mandibles to inflict a painful bite on any predator that threatens them. *Ouch!*

When the time is right, the large larvae crawl out of the water and dig underground chambers, where they turn into pupae.

FACTS

OTHER COMMON NAME Dobsonfly

SCIENTIFIC NAME *Corydalus cornutus* / Family: Corydalidae

SIZE Up to 5.5 inches (140 mm), not including male's mandibles

WINGS Yes

FOOD Adult: does not eat / Larva: aquatic insects and small fish

HABITAT Near rivers and streams

RANGE Eastern parts of North America

The adult male dobsonfly's pincers **LOOK THREATENING, BUT THEY'RE ONLY USED DURING MATING.** Females, on the other hand, use their shorter pincers to bite.

ANTLION
FAMILY MYRMELEONTIDAE

Antlion larvae, sometimes called doodlebugs, are cunning predators with huge sickle-shaped jaws. In some species, the larva creates a pitfall trap to capture prey. It digs a sand pit and buries itself in the middle, just under the surface. Its wide-open jaws face upward to catch insects, especially ants that stumble into the sand trap. There are about 2,000 species of antlions worldwide; they are especially common in semi-arid areas.

All adult antlion species look a little like damselflies (see pages 68–71) but with thicker, clubbed antennae. Females lay their eggs in the sand or dust. When a larva matures, it makes a silk and sand cocoon underground and then transforms into a pupa. When the adult emerges, it climbs to the surface and flies in search of a mate.

FACTS

OTHER COMMON NAME Doodlebug

SCIENTIFIC NAME Family: Myrmeleontidae

SIZE 1.75 inches (45 mm)

WINGS Yes

FOOD Adult: occasionally eats nectar, pollen, and insects / Larva: ants and other small insects

HABITAT Dry locations with fine sand or dust

RANGE Worldwide

In the United States, antlions are **OFTEN CALLED DOODLEBUGS** because their **LARVAE MAKE DOODLE-LIKE IMPRESSIONS** in the surface of the sand as they search for a new place to make a sand pit.

COMMON GREEN LACEWING

FAMILY CHRYSOPIDAE

Like lace bugs (see pages 136–137), the green lacewing has netlike patterns on its wings that resemble lace. The green lacewing's wings aren't just pretty; they serve an important function by helping the insect avoid bats.

Bats are major predators of the green lacewings. When these winged mammals are on the hunt, they emit sound waves that travel through the air. When the waves hit an object—like a lacewing—they bounce back to the bat. This tells the bat where the object (in this case, its prey) is located.

Fortunately the green lacewing has ears at the base of its forewings that pick up vibrations. These vibrations usually give the lacewing enough time to dodge the flying mammal.

FACTS

COMMON NAME Common green lacewing

SCIENTIFIC NAME Family: Chrysopidae

SIZE 0.6–0.8 inch (15–20 mm)

WINGS Yes

FOOD Adult: pollen, nectar, and honeydew / Larva: insects including aphids, leafhoppers, moths, and caterpillars

HABITAT Open fields with plenty of vegetation

RANGE Worldwide except Antarctica

Lacewing larvae feed on various soft-bodied insects, especially aphids. For that reason, they're **SOMETIMES CALLED "APHID LIONS."** A larva measures only 0.5 inch (12 mm), but can eat about **200 APHIDS IN JUST ONE WEEK!**

SNAKEFLY
FAMILIES RAPHIDIIDAE AND INOCELLIIDAE

Back in the Jurassic period (140 million years ago), snakeflies were very common on Earth. Now only two families with about 260 species are left, but they still look like the fossilized snakeflies from the Jurassic period. That's why today's snakeflies are considered living fossils.

Snakeflies have a long, snakelike thorax (the midsection of their bodies) that resembles a neck. Their two pairs of long, thin wings are transparent. Females have a needlelike tube called an ovipositor that may look like a stinger but is used only for laying eggs.

Larvae hang out under the bark of trees, and in leaf litter, crevices, and debris. Adults are territorial and carnivorous. They are excellent at pest control because they eat aphids and small beetle larvae that can damage crops and trees.

Modern snakeflies **LOOK A LOT LIKE THIS FOSSIL SNAKEFLY** (*Ohmella coffini*) from the Miocene epoch. It was found in stone in southern France.

A female snakefly hunts aphids on a stem.

TARANTULA HAWK
FAMILY POMPILIDAE

Tarantula hawks are huge wasps that can deliver a walloping sting. Most predatory animals won't touch them.

To reproduce, the female tarantula hawk finds and stings a tarantula and then drags it, sometimes over long distances, to her burrow or a specially prepared nest. She lays a single egg on the abdomen of the paralyzed tarantula, then buries it alive. After hatching, the wasp larva eats the inside of the spider. At first, it avoids the spider's vital organs. This delays the spider's death, and thus gives the wasp time to develop.

Male tarantula hawks search for mates by hilltopping. They sit on tall plants on hills and watch for passing females that are ready to mate.

FACTS

COMMON NAME Tarantula hawk

SCIENTIFIC NAME Family: Pompilidae

SIZE About 0.5–2.25 inches (12–57 mm) (for the genus *Pepsis*)

WINGS Yes

FOOD Adult: nectar, pollen, and fruit juice / Larva: tarantulas and other large, juicy spiders

HABITAT Where tarantulas are found, from rainforests to deserts

RANGE India, Southeast Asia, Australia, Europe, Africa, and the Americas

One easy way to tell tarantula hawk males and females apart is to look at their antennae. **THE MALE'S ANTENNAE ARE STRAIGHT AND THE FEMALE'S ARE COILED NEAR THE TIPS.** Only the female tarantula hawk has a stinger. It's the same organ (ovipositor) that she uses to lay eggs.

This paper wasp works on building the cells of its nest. Some paper wasp nests contain 200 cells.

PAPER WASP

FAMILY VESPIDAE

Paper wasps are the builders of the insect world, with a real knack for nest construction. To build their nests, most paper wasp species begin by gathering fibers from branches and dead plants. They mix the materials together with their saliva, then shape the mixture into clusters of comb-shaped cells. When the nest cells dry, they have a paperlike quality. The nests are also water-repellent, which keeps them dry in the rain. The wasps build their nests in sheltered areas, including tree branches and the eaves of houses. For added protection, the wasps secrete a chemical around their nest. The chemical repels ants that would otherwise feed on the eggs stored inside the nest.

FACTS

OTHER COMMON NAME Umbrella wasp

SCIENTIFIC NAME Subfamily: Polistinae / Family: Vespidae

SIZE Under 0.7–1 inch (18–25 mm)

WINGS Yes

FOOD Adult: nectar and honeydew / Larva: insects such as caterpillars

HABITAT Urban areas, meadows, and grasslands

RANGE Worldwide

Scientists have discovered that **ONE PAPER WASP SPECIES,** *Polistes fuscatus,* **CAN RECOGNIZE INDIVIDUALS OF ITS TYPE BY THE PATTERNS ON THEIR FACES.** Their ability to recognize faces is much like our own ability to do so!

EASTERN YELLOW JACKET

FAMILY VESPIDAE

Eastern yellow jacket adults prefer to eat sugary treats such as nectar, but when it comes to feeding their young, only meat will do.

After their larvae hatch from the eggs, the adult seeks out an insect, such as a caterpillar, or a nice, juicy spider. The yellow jacket uses its legs to grab the spider and stings it if it puts up a fight. Once the spider is firmly in its grip, the yellow jacket rips off the spider's cephalothorax (head-thorax) and legs. Then, it sinks its mouthparts into what's left of the spider's body to suck out its insides.

Next, the yellow jacket drags the spider's remains to the nest. There, it vomits the contents of its digested meal for the newly hatched larvae to feed on. After a few days, when the larvae are older, they feed on solid pieces of the prey.

FACTS

COMMON NAME Eastern yellow jacket

SCIENTIFIC NAME *Vespula maculifrons* / Family: Vespidae

SIZE About 0.49–0.71 inch (12.5–18 mm), depending on its caste

WINGS Yes

FOOD Adult: sugary foods such as nectar / Larva: spiders and insects

HABITAT Cities, suburbs, and farmland

RANGE Eastern North America, as well as the Great Plains of the United States

Some yellow jacket **NESTS CAN BE HUGE.** In 2006, a man in Tallassee, Alabama, U.S.A., discovered a yellow jacket nest that was **SO LARGE IT FILLED HIS ENTIRE CAR!**

This eastern yellow jacket returns to its nest with a piece of meat in its jaws.

That's
Fact-tastic!

Some farmers and orchard growers use **BIOLOGICAL CONTROL TO REDUCE POPULATIONS OF INSECTS THAT DAMAGE THEIR CROPS.** Certain species of ichneumon wasps are selected as **BIOCONTROL AGENTS** for their ability to attack specific types of pest insects without killing beneficial insects. **IT'S A WIN-WIN SITUATION** for both people and parasitoid wasps.

The female ichneumon wasp uses her long ovipositor to drill a hole into wood.

ICHNEUMON WASP
FAMILY ICHNEUMONIDAE

Female ichneumon wasps have what look like long, painful stingers, but in fact they're harmless—to people, that is. Their superlong tube is an ovipositor, used for laying eggs on or inside a host. Some ichneumon wasps even use their ovipositor to drill through wood to reach hosts hidden inside branches and tree trunks. Ichneumon wasps are parasitoids on the larvae, pupae, and nymphs of other insects, like butterflies, moths, beetles, bees, and aphids. Some even deposit their eggs inside spiders. When the wasp's larvae hatch from the eggs, they devour their host!

With some 60,000 named species, ichneumon wasps make up the largest family in the world. They are slender-bodied, with long antennae. Male ichneumons do not have an ovipositor or stinger, and they tend to be smaller than the females.

FACTS

OTHER COMMON NAMES Ichneumonid wasp, Darwin's wasp

SCIENTIFIC NAME Family: Ichneumonidae

SIZE Less than an inch to about 2 inches (51 mm)

WINGS Yes

FOOD Adult: nectar and plant sap / Larva: immature forms of various insects and spiders

HABITAT Wherever the wasps can find their host

RANGE Worldwide except Antarctica

As the **FEMALE AT LEFT DEPOSITS HER EGGS,** a pouch at the tip of her abdomen keeps her ovipositor steady.

OAK APPLE GALL WASP

FAMILY CYNIPIDAE

Like many insects, female gall wasps lay their eggs on plant leaves. But after the eggs hatch, something strange happens. The larvae trigger a chemical reaction in the plant. The plant tissues begin to grow and form a protective covering over the newly hatched larvae. The covering is called a gall.

Galls can vary in shape and size, depending on the species they house. A gall produced by an oak apple gall wasp is about two inches (50 mm) wide and is shaped like an apple. The gall provides the wasp larva with nutrients as it develops inside. When the wasp becomes an adult, it bores a hole through the gall and emerges.

FACTS

COMMON NAME Oak apple gall wasp

SCIENTIFIC NAME *Amphibolips confluenta* / Family: Cynipidae

SIZE Under 0.25 inch (6 mm)

WINGS Yes

FOOD Adult: does not feed and lives only for about one week / Larva: plant tissue inside the gall

HABITAT Wherever red, black, and scarlet oaks are found

RANGE Eastern North America

Wasps have a **NARROW JUNCTION BETWEEN THEIR THORAX AND ABDOMEN,** which gives them the appearance of having a narrow waist. **THIS "WASP WAIST" WAS THE INSPIRATION FOR A ONCE POPULAR FASHION CONCEPT** that began in the 1800s: Women used supertight corsets to draw in their waists.

This gall, which looks like an apple, contains a developing larva.

That's Fact-tastic!
When velvet ants are THREATENED, THEY MAKE A SQUEAKING SOUND by rubbing two parts of their body together. FEMALES CAN ALSO DELIVER A STING that's lethal to some insects. The sting is so painful that the wasps are sometimes called "cow killers." However, there is NO EVIDENCE OF A VELVET ANT EVER KILLING A COW!

RED VELVET ANT
FAMILY MUTILLIDAE

Red velvet ants aren't really ants. They're actually wasps, but the female members of the group have wingless, ant-shaped bodies. Males, on the other hand, have wings.

Both females and males are covered with dense velvety bristles that give them a soft appearance. However, the opposite is actually true. Red velvet ants have a very tough exoskeleton. This trait prevents them from losing moisture in the dry areas that they inhabit. It also helps protect them from the stings of bumblebees and other wasps.

Why would bumblebees and other wasps attack the velvet ants? Female velvet ants have been known to crawl into these insects' nests and deposit their eggs there. When larvae hatch from the eggs, they have instant access to their prey.

FACTS

OTHER COMMON NAME Eastern velvet ant

SCIENTIFIC NAME *Dasymutilla occidentalis /* Family: Mutillidae

SIZE Up to 0.75 inch (19 mm)

WINGS Present only in males

FOOD Adult: nectar / Larva: larvae of other insects

HABITAT Meadows, fields, edge of forests

RANGE United States: eastern states south of New England and Gulf states

WASPS
GALLERY

Scientists divide wasps into two main groups: social and solitary. Social wasps live together in colonies that consist of a queen, workers, and drones. The drones and queen mate to produce young. The queen is responsible for nest construction, which she continues to work on until she is ready to lay her eggs. At that point, the workers take over the nest-building duties. The workers also feed the young larvae after they have hatched from the eggs.

Unlike social wasps, solitary wasps live alone. Most solitary wasps are parasitoids whose young feed on their hosts—usually insects or spiders.

There are some 100,000 known species of wasps in the world with thousands more not yet named. The unnamed ones are mostly extremely tiny—hard or impossible to see and even harder to study. In the past, scientists hadn't focused on finding nearly invisible wasps, but with newer collection techniques available the number of known wasp species will keep growing. To get a sense of just how varied wasps are, check out the critters shown here.

This paper wasp works on constructing the hexagon-shaped cells of its nest. Eventually, each cell will house one egg.

A wasp ovipositor can double as a stinger.

The potter wasp zips back to its nest with a tasty caterpillar. The wasp itself won't eat the caterpillar. Instead, it will leave it for one of its developing larvae to eat.

This paper nest created by hornets is anchored to a tree branch. A large entrance is located on the bottom.

This wasp is chomping on wood. It will chew the wood into a pasty pulp, which it will use to build its nest.

This Tinkerbell wasp is extremely tiny, at only 0.0098 inch (0.25 mm) long. Its wings are like feathers, and it feeds on tiny insect eggs.

WESTERN HONEYBEE
FAMILY APIDAE

Acolony of honeybees live together in a hive, where they have many responsibilities that range from collecting nectar and pollen to hive construction. Most of the work is done by the colony's female worker bees.

A worker bee travels from flower to flower in search of pollen and nectar. The pollen gets stuck on the bee's body hairs. Then the bee brushes the pollen into structures on its hind legs, called pollen baskets, and stores the nectar in a special pouch. Back at the hive, the pollen and nectar are processed by another group of worker bees to make honey.

The workers are also in charge of building the hive's cells, or rooms. They build these six-sided cells from a waxy substance secreted from their bodies. The cells are used to store honey and to house developing larvae and pupae.

In addition, the workers tend to the queen bee, which mates with males called drones to produce the eggs. The workers feed the queen bee "royal jelly," a mixture that includes proteins, sugar, and fatty acids. They also provide food for her larvae.

FACTS

OTHER COMMON NAME European honeybee

SCIENTIFIC NAME *Apis mellifera* / Family: Apidae

SIZE Workers: 0.4–0.7 inch (10–18 mm) / Queens: 0.7–0.8 inch (18–20 mm) / Drones: 0.59–0.67 inch (15–17 mm)

WINGS Yes

FOOD Adult: pollen, nectar, honey, and in some cases, secretions called royal jelly / Larva: royal jelly and beebread (a mixture of bitter pollen and honey)

HABITAT Areas with flowering plants, such as meadows and gardens

RANGE Worldwide

That's Fact-tastic!

When a worker honeybee locates a food source, she **RETURNS TO THE HIVE TO SHARE THE NEWS.** She **PERFORMS A WAGGLE DANCE** or a circle dance to let her nest mates know **WHERE TO FIND A GOOD FOOD SOURCE.** She also **REGURGITATES SOME NECTAR** from her honey stomach for **OTHER BEES TO LEARN THE TASTE** of the nectar in a flower patch.

In the photo above, the yellow mass on the bee's leg is the pollen.

Unlike other male bee species, which have yellow facial hair, the male buff-tailed bumblebee has black hair on its face.

That's Fact-tastic!

BUMBLEBEES ARE NOT AGGRESSIVE and so are not likely to sting, except very close to their nest. ONLY THE QUEEN AND WORKER BEES CAN STING. A bumblebee's stinger is smooth, and the bee CAN STING MORE THAN ONCE, UNLIKE A HONEYBEE, which has a barbed stinger and stings only once, then dies.

BUFF-TAILED BUMBLEBEE

FAMILY APIDAE

Like honeybees, buff-tailed bumblebees travel among flowers collecting nectar—and sometimes pollen—to produce honey (photo below). But this bumblebee species differs from its honeybee cousin in many ways. Unlike honeybees, which live in hives aboveground, buff-tailed bumblebee colonies reside in underground nests. Often, the nests are housed in former mouse burrows.

Unlike honeybees, which stay alive year round, most buff-tailed bumblebees can survive only during warmer months. Why? The bees need to heat their bodies in order to fly. They can generate some heat by shivering, but rely mainly on the sun's warm rays to do the job. This becomes difficult when temperatures dip in late fall and early winter. When the bumblebee is unable to fly, it can't collect food, and therefore starves.

The queen buff-tailed bumblebee is typically the only member of her hive to survive the winter. She hibernates until spring and then starts a new colony.

FACTS

OTHER COMMON NAMES Large earth bumblebee, humble-bee

SCIENTIFIC NAME *Bombus terrestris* / Family: Apidae

SIZE 0.6–1 inch (15–25 mm)

WINGS Yes

FOOD Adult and larva: pollen and nectar

HABITAT Edge of forests, in meadows and grasslands

RANGE Europe, North Africa, parts of Asia, New Zealand, and Australia (in Tasmania)

NEON CUCKOO BEE

FAMILY APIDAE

Cuckoo birds have a bad reputation for laying their eggs in the nests of other birds—and the cuckoo bee is no different.

The neon cuckoo bee sneaks into the nest of the blue-banded bee, usually while its hosts are out collecting nectar and pollen for their own colony. The cuckoo bee then lays its eggs, as well as a food supply, inside the cells that house the colony's own eggs. When the cuckoo larvae hatch, they attack and kill the blue-banded bee colony's larvae and feed on the food inside the cells.

Sometimes, the blue-banded bees are actually present when the cuckoo bee sneaks in. Since the bees are similar in color, the invader can go undetected by the colony.

FACTS

COMMON NAME Neon cuckoo bee

SCIENTIFIC NAME *Thyreus nitidulus* / Family: Apidae

SIZE 0.4–0.6 inch (10–14 mm)

WINGS Yes

FOOD Adult: pollen and nectar / Larva: larvae of other bees, pollen, and nectar

HABITAT Woodlands and urban areas

RANGE Throughout most of Australia; New Guinea

That's
Fact-tastic!

TO GAIN CONTROL
OF THE HOST NEST, some
cuckoo bee species will KILL
THE QUEEN. They then use
physical attacks or their
pheromones (chemicals that
influence behavior) to
CONTROL THE NEST'S
WORKERS.

This bulldog ant
leans over to take
a sip of water.

BULLDOG ANT
FAMILY FORMICIDAE

Australia's bulldog ants are some of the largest ants in the world. An adult bulldog ant can measure 1.6 inches (40 mm) long.

Bulldog ants are as ferocious as they are big. They have sharp serrated jaws and a powerful sting, which they'll use against anything that gets in their way. But their main target is their prey.

A bulldog ant is typically an ambush hunter. It remains hidden, sometimes under a leaf, until it sees its prey walk by. At that instant, the ant leaps onto its victim's back and stabs it with its stinger. Ouch!

The bulldog ant then feeds on the animal's juices and drags the carcass back to its nest. There, ant larvae consume the remains.

FACTS

OTHER COMMON NAMES Bull ant, Jumper ant, Inch ant

SCIENTIFIC NAME *Myrmecia* / Family: Formicidae

SIZE Up to 1.6 inches (40 mm)

WINGS Present in some species

FOOD Adult: small insects, honeydew, seeds, and fungi / Larva: dead insects

HABITAT Urban areas, forests, woodland, heath

RANGE Australia and New Caledonia

Bulldog ants have **AMAZING JUMPING ABILITIES.** The ants are known to **POUNCE ON FLYING INSECTS,** such as wasps!

WEAVER ANT
FAMILY FORMICIDAE

Weaver ant colonies live in leafy nests located in the trees of Africa, Australia, and Asia. To build these nests, the ants rely on the colony's larvae.

Weaver ant larvae secrete a sticky silklike substance from their heads. Adults use this substance like glue. While a few worker ants hold together two leaves, a third worker gently holds a larva with its mandibles (photo below). The worker then taps the larva on the head with its antenna, signaling for it to produce the "glue." When the larva secretes the substance, the workers use it to seal the leaves together. The workers and larvae continue this process until they have built a nest.

OTHER COMMON NAMES Green tree ant, Asian weaver ant

SCIENTIFIC NAME *Oecophylla smaragdina* / Family: Formicidae

SIZE Workers: 0.3–0.4 inch (8–10 mm) / Queens: 0.7–0.8 inch (18–20 mm) / Drones: 0.39–0.43 (10–11 mm)

WINGS Queen has wings, which she sheds

FOOD Adult: mainly nectar and honeydew / Larva: secretions from the queen ant and regurgitated food

HABITAT Forested areas

RANGE Africa, Australia, and Asia

Weaver ant nests aren't just populated by weaver ants. The **CATERPILLAR OF A CERTAIN BUTTERFLY SPECIES (LIPHYRA BRASSOLIS) MIGHT ALSO RESIDE IN THE NEST.** The thick-skinned caterpillar **FEEDS ON THE ANTS' EGGS AND LARVAE.** Often, the ants fight back, but they are unable to defeat their unwelcome houseguests.

This leafcutter ant uses
its mandibles to cut off
a piece of leaf.

LEAFCUTTER ANT
FAMILY FORMICIDAE

Leafcutter ants are the gardeners of the insect world. However, these social insects don't help plants to grow. Instead, they grow a type of fungus, which they eat. How do they do it?

First, worker ants find leaves that will help their fungus garden grow. As they travel in a line through the forest, they leave behind a scent trail. The scent helps them find their way back home.

When the ants come upon a group of leafy plants, they get to work. They use their mandibles, or jaws, to cut the leaves, flowers, and stems into pieces, then carry them back to their nest.

In the nest, a different group of workers chew the leaves and plant parts into a pulp and deposit it onto the fungus garden. The pulp helps the fungus grow, so the ants will have plenty to eat.

The leafcutter ants are very protective of their food supply. When they detect any disease-causing microorganisms on the fungus, the ants remove the infested fungus, along with other waste, and place them in a special waste chamber or in a heap outside the nest.

FACTS

COMMON NAME Leafcutter ant

SCIENTIFIC NAME *Atta* / Family: Formicidae

SIZE Workers: 0.08–0.6 inch (2–15 mm) / Queens: 0.9 inch (22 mm) / Males: 0.7 inch (18 mm)

WINGS Yes

FOOD Adult: fungus / Larva: regurgitated food

HABITAT Rainforest floor

RANGE Louisiana and Texas, U.S.A.; Central and South America

The **SMALLEST WORKER ANTS,** called minims, are responsible for **FEEDING THE LARGER WORKERS AND PROTECTING THEM FROM PARASITES.** They often **HITCH A RIDE ON THE LEAVES** that other members carry. The largest worker ants, called majors, aggressively protect the colony with their huge, sharp mandibles (see page 34).

RED FIRE ANT
FAMILY FORMICIDAE

Red fire ants are notorious pests. They attack and kill small animals including bees, birds, native ants, and pets. They also attack people and cattle, occasionally causing them to die. People living in areas with red fire ants know to watch where they walk or sit down when they are outdoors.

These ants will bite to get a grip on the skin, then inject a venom from their stinger (on the abdomen) that burns. This is how they got their name—fire ant. Originally, the red fire ant came from South America, but it has been accidentally introduced in many places around the world. These ants build large mounds in open areas. They also colonize moist places near rivers, streams, and watered lawns. They find shelter under rocks, logs, bricks, and wood.

Each year, these ants can cause billions of U.S. dollars in crop damage, home damage, and more. They also cause damage to the environment by driving out native species.

FACTS

OTHER COMMON NAME Red imported fire ant

SCIENTIFIC NAME *Solenopsis invicta* / Family: Formicidae

SIZE Workers: about 0.04–0.2 inch (1–4 mm) / Queens: about 0.28–0.3 inch (7–7.5 mm) / Males: about 0.24 inch (6 mm)

WINGS Only in males (drones) and queens

FOOD Insects, dead animals, seeds, and plants

HABITAT A wide variety of habitats such as meadows, parks, lawns, pastures, and agricultural lands

RANGE Warm and humid regions worldwide

Following hurricanes and floods, colonies of red fire ants **SURVIVE BY LINKING LEGS AND FORMING FLOATING RAFTS** on the water's surface. Their numbers can be in the **HUNDREDS OF THOUSANDS.** Once the raft floats to land, the ants disembark and make a new home.

DOG AND CAT FLEA

FAMILY PULICIDAE

Does your dog or cat have an itch it just can't scratch? If so, it may have fleas. As these tiny parasites feed on your pet's blood, they produce saliva that can irritate the dog or cat's skin. And it seems like no amount of scratching can get rid of the flea. Why?

One reason is the flea's cling-on ability. The flea's joints are covered with spines. The spines work like a comb or the bristles of a brush to help the flea cling onto fur, even when the dog or cat makes sudden movements.

In addition, the flea has amazing jumping abilities—thanks largely to its pleural arch, a structure in its hind legs made of elastic protein. The arch is usually compressed, but when the flea's hind muscles relax, it is released. This allows the flea to take a high-flying leap—and dodge your pet's scratching leg.

FACTS

COMMON NAMES Dog flea, cat flea

SCIENTIFIC NAME *Ctenocephalides canis* and *C. felis* / Family: Pulicidae

SIZE 0.06–0.08 inch (1.5–2 mm)

WINGS No

FOOD Adult: blood of dogs, cats, and sometimes humans / Larva: adult flea feces, as well as dead skin and food particles

HABITAT In dog and cat fur

RANGE Worldwide

Fleas are able to **JUMP HORIZONTALLY UP TO 13 INCHES** (33 cm) and **VERTICALLY UP TO SEVEN INCHES** (18 cm). In the insect world, only the froghopper can reach a greater height relative to body length with one leap.

This photo shows what a cat flea looks like under a scanning electron microscope. Studies show that young cats have more fleas than older ones—most likely because they have poorer grooming habits.

A hangingfly in its typical resting position

That's
Fact-tastic!

Hangingflies **AREN'T THE ONLY "BUGS" THAT GIVE NUPTIAL GIFTS.** For example, some male flies, butterflies, crickets, katydids, and spiders also give **NUTRITIOUS GIFTS TO THEIR INTENDED MATES.**

HANGINGFLY
FAMILY BITTACIDAE

Hangingflies might look like crane flies (see pages 224–225), but they have four wings instead of two. They hang from leaves by their two front legs and grasp passing insects for a meal with their other four legs. Their legs are long and slender, but very strong. Oddly, they can't walk at all. They are only able to fly or hang.

Hangingflies fly like crane flies with slow, flapping wing beats. They are often attracted to lights, and if they're disturbed, they will fly away. Just like crane flies, hangingflies can be mistaken for mosquitoes when they flap around lights at night. They are easy to tell apart by their long snout with mouthparts on the end.

Hangingflies may be most famous for the nuptial gift males present to females before mating. The gift is a nutritious meal of another insect. The larger the gift, the more likely it is that the female will accept his gift and mate with him.

FACTS

OTHER COMMON NAME Hanging scorpionflies

SCIENTIFIC NAME Family: Bittacidae

SIZE 0.24–0.39 inch (6–10 mm)

WINGS Yes (two forewings and two hind wings)

FOOD Adult: flying insects and caterpillars / Larva: unknown

HABITAT Woodlands, especially near streams and moist environments

RANGE Worldwide

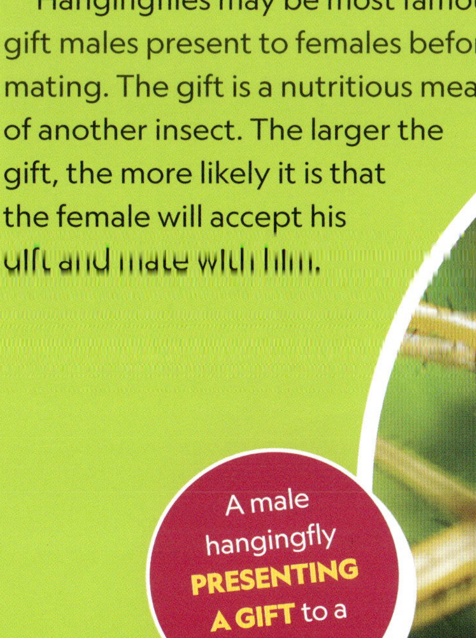

TWISTED-WING PARASITE

FAMILY STYLOPIDIA

Twisted-wing parasites in the family Stylopidia commonly feed on bees and wasps. The adult male parasite has eyes, legs, antennae, and twisted hind wings. The female, however, has none of these. She lives inside her host where she feeds on it. A small part of her body sticks out between her host's abdominal segments. She emits a pheromone, a chemical released to send messages, that wafts in the air to attract a winged male. After mating, the fertilized eggs hatch inside the female and the tiny larvae feed on her body from the inside, killing her. The larvae then leave to quickly find a new host bee or wasp to live in. The larvae latch onto their host and secrete an enzyme that softens the host's tough exoskeleton, allowing the larvae to enter. Amazingly, the bee or wasp host usually survives being parasitized.

FACTS

OTHER COMMON NAME Stylops

SCIENTIFIC NAME Family: Stylopidia

SIZE Genus *Stylops*: 0.08–0.12 inch (2–3 mm)

WINGS Only in males

FOOD Adult male: does not eat / Adult female and larva: feed on host insect

HABITAT Inside the host insect and the area around the host

RANGE Worldwide except Antarctica

Three **FEMALE TWISTED-WING PARASITES STICK OUT** from the segments of a wasp's abdomen.

The **ADULT MALE** twisted-wing parasite can be very **HARD TO FIND** because **HE TYPICALLY LIVES ONLY A FEW HOURS.** During that time, he rushes to find a female partner to mate with and start another generation. **HE HAS NO FUNCTIONAL MOUTHPARTS, SO HE CAN'T FEED.**

A male twisted-wing parasite mating with a female

A female mosquito fills up on a person's blood. She'll leave when she's full.

MOSQUITO
FAMILY CULICIDAE

In most of the 3,500-plus species found worldwide, the female mosquito is a bloodthirsty pest. She requires an occasional blood meal in order to get enough nutrients to make her eggs.

The mosquito uses her keen sense of smell to search for warm-blooded vertebrates, including people. She is able to detect exhaled carbon dioxide and chemicals in a person's sweat. When the female mosquito takes a blood meal, she injects saliva in order to prevent the blood from clogging her proboscis. The proboscis is like a syringe—long and hollow.

Mosquitoes are mostly active at dawn and dusk. People need to be especially cautious at those times, as some mosquitoes carry infectious diseases and parasites that they transfer to human hosts—diseases such as malaria, yellow fever, dengue fever, West Nile virus, and Zika virus. About 500,000 people die each year from mosquito-borne diseases.

FACTS

COMMON NAME Mosquito

SCIENTIFIC NAME Family: Culicidae

SIZE 0.125–0.75 inch (3–20 mm)

WINGS Yes (front wings for flying and hind wings, called halteres, for balancing)

FOOD Adult: nectar, honeydew, water, and the female takes blood meals / Larva: algae, bacteria, and various microbes

HABITAT Moist soils, standing water (tree holes, woodland pools, and swamps)

RANGE Worldwide

Both male and female mosquitoes **DRINK SUGAR-RICH NECTAR** from flowers and honeydew from bugs. **SOME ARE EVEN POLLINATORS.**

MARSH CRANE FLY

FAMILY TIPULIDAE

It's easy to confuse the marsh crane fly for a giant mosquito. Crane flies have long, spindly legs and thin abdomens like a mosquito. But they are different. Unlike mosquitoes, the crane fly is a poor flier and wobbles in flight, and these flies don't bite people. However, larval crane flies are destructive to our food supply. They eat the roots of cereal crops, potatoes, cabbage, raspberries, strawberries, onions, garlic, clover, and grasses. In contrast, many adults don't feed at all!

The marsh crane fly also differs from mosquitoes in its egg-laying methods. Most mosquitoes deposit their eggs on the water's surface, but the crane fly prefers soil. To lay eggs, the female aims her pointy abdomen straight down and hops along the soil, laying an egg each time she lands. When the larvae hatch from their eggs, they go to work eating the roots of young plants.

FACTS

COMMON NAME Marsh crane fly

SCIENTIFIC NAME *Tipula oleracea* / Family: Tipulidae

SIZE Body length up to 1.02 inches (26 mm)

WINGS Yes (front wings for flying and hind wings, called halteres, for balancing)

FOOD Adult: does not eat / Larva: grass roots, cereal crops, potatoes, cabbages, raspberries, strawberries, clover, onions, and garlic

HABITAT Gardens, pastures, meadows, and moist places

RANGE North America, Canada, Europe, Asia, Arabian Peninsula, North Africa, and Ecuador

The front wings of this crane fly lie closed over its back. Looking like little knobs on a thread, **THE MODIFIED HIND WINGS** (called halteres) keep the fly **BALANCED IN FLIGHT.**

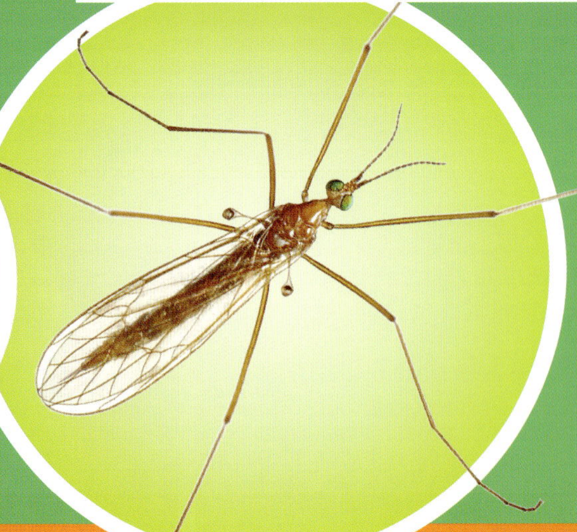

ONE WORD OR TWO?

You'll see common names like crane fly and fruit fly in which "fly" is a separate word. You'll also see combined names like mayfly, dragonfly, caddisfly, and dobsonfly. **IF "FLY" IS A SEPARATE WORD, IT BELONGS TO THE ORDER DIPTERA ("TRUE FLIES").** Otherwise it belongs to a different order.

NEW ZEALAND GLOWWORM

FAMILY KEROPLATIDAE

The larvae of the New Zealand glowworm live on the ceilings of caves and other damp, dark places. They make silk "fishing lines" dotted with tiny blobs of glue to trap flying insects, their food. The best part is they glow in the dark—much the same way as firefly larvae. However, this glowworm is a fly, not a beetle like the firefly. Its glow is so bright that it lights up the dangling sticky lines.

The New Zealand glowworms attract more than prey with their light. They are a major tourist attraction too. One of the best known places to see them is the Waitomo Caves on the North Island of New Zealand.

Their scientific name means "glowing spider-worm," because they hunt with silk, like spiders do. The name given to the creatures by the Native Maori people is *titiwai*, meaning "lights reflected in water." As adults, glowworms are called fungus gnats.

FACTS

OTHER COMMON NAME *Titiwai*

SCIENTIFIC NAME *Arachnocampa luminosa* / Family: Keroplatidae

SIZE 0.5–0.6 inch (13–15 mm), larva up to 1.6 inches (40 mm)

WINGS Yes

FOOD Adult: does not eat / Larva: flying insects, like midges, mayflies, and crane flies, caught in the larva's sticky silk lines

HABITAT Caves, grottoes, and damp, dark, protected places in the forest

RANGE New Zealand

This glowworm pupa hangs from silk threads. When the larvae become **PUPAE,** they **STILL GLOW PART OF THE TIME.** When a **FEMALE PUPA** is about to turn into an adult, her **GLOW INCREASES**—and that attracts potential mates. But the males must wait around until she transforms into an adult.

MEDITERRANEAN FRUIT FLY
FAMILY TEPHRITIDAE

As with all fruit flies, the larvae of a Mediterranean fruit fly (nicknamed "medfly") develop in moist places where there is water and organic matter that is rich in nutrients from dead organisms.

The female members of the family have a sharp ovipositor, which they use to pierce the skin of fruit and lay their eggs inside. Species like the medfly aren't too picky about the fruit they select. It can include apricots, avocados, grapefruit, and tomatoes. This has caused problems for farmers all over the world.

Fruits containing medfly larvae ship to other countries. After the larvae hatch from their eggs, they invade the crops of their new homes, becoming an invasive species.

Today, the medfly is a huge problem in Hawaii, U.S.A., where it has destroyed a variety of crops, including papaya and guava.

FACTS

OTHER COMMON NAME Medfly

SCIENTIFIC NAME *Ceratitis capitata* / Family: Tephritidae

SIZE 0.12–0.2 inch (3–5 mm)

WINGS Yes

FOOD Adult: juices of ripe and decomposing fruits, and bird feces / Larva: fruits and some vegetables

HABITAT Wide-ranging, including forests, open woodland, and coasts

RANGE Worldwide

A medfly larva, also called a maggot, **FEEDS ON THE ROTTING FRUIT IN WHICH IT WAS LAID.**

ANOTHER FRUIT FLY (*Zonosemata vittigera*) from the same family **IMITATES A JUMPING SPIDER TO PROTECT ITSELF** from being eaten by the spiders. The fly **HAS WHAT LOOKS LIKE A SPIDER LEG PATTERN ON ITS WINGS,** which it waves to mimic a jumping spider's combative dance. When the spider sees the fly displaying, it displays in turn, then retreats.

That's
Fact-tastic!
The MORE BLOOD a female
biting midge consumes, the
MORE EGGS SHE WILL
PRODUCE. One species,
Culicoides furens, CAN LAY
UP TO 110 EGGS after
a blood meal.

BITING MIDGE
FAMILY CERATOPOGONIDAE

Biting midges are tiny insects, measuring only 0.04 to 0.12 inch (1–3 mm) long. Their tiny size is the reason why they are sometimes called no-see-ums.

Like mosquitoes, female midges need to feed on blood in order to get enough protein in their diet to produce their eggs. To get blood, they'll bite any organism they come across. That includes other insects and mammals—and humans, too.

Unlike mosquitoes, biting midges don't pierce the skin. Instead, they use their scissorlike mouthparts to cut it open. After the cut is made, the midge injects an anticlotting chemical into the blood to ensure it flows freely. At that point, the midge is ready to suck.

FACTS

OTHER COMMON NAME No-see-um

SCIENTIFIC NAME *Leptoconops* / Family: Ceratopogonidae

SIZE 0.04–0.12 inch (1–3 mm)

WINGS Yes (front wings for flying and hind wings, called halteres, for balancing)

FOOD Adult: blood (females only) and nectar / Larva. small organisms, some species feed on bacteria, fungi, and algae

HABITAT Common in salt marshes and tropical areas, and in rotting fruit

RANGE Tropical and subtropical areas

FLESH FLY

FAMILY SARCOPHAGIDAE

Flesh flies belong to a family of insects called Sarcophagidae. The name, which is made up of the Greek words for "flesh" and "eating," refers to the fly's tendency to feed on dead animals (called carrion). This includes insects, snails, and amphibians, such as frogs and toads.

The flesh fly also uses the carrion as a host for its developing larvae. The female produces eggs inside her body. After they hatch, she deposits them into the body of the animal, where they mature. The host animal is usually dead, but there are a few exceptions. One species, *Sarcophaga kellyi,* deposits its larvae onto a live grasshopper. The little maggots then burrow into the insect and feed on its organs. They remain inside the grasshopper until they are ready to enter the pupal stage. At that point, they make their exit and drop into the soil.

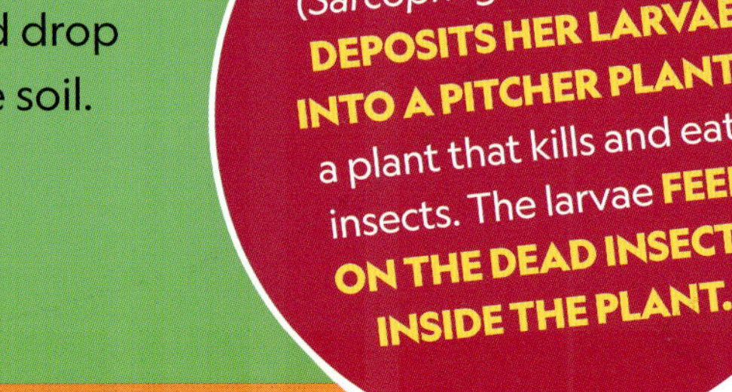

The Eastern flesh fly (*Sarcophaga sarraceniae*) **DEPOSITS HER LARVAE INTO A PITCHER PLANT—** a plant that kills and eats insects. The larvae **FEED ON THE DEAD INSECTS INSIDE THE PLANT.**

The flesh fly can be distinguished from the common house fly by the stripes on its thorax. The flesh fly has three dark stripes while the house fly has four.

That's
Fact-tastic!

Many caddisfly larvae **BUILD A PROTECTIVE CASE** around themselves by secreting a sticky silk and **DECORATING IT WITH MATERIALS SUCH AS SAND, GRAVEL, AND DEBRIS.** Some people take advantage of the caddisfly's natural ability by having captive larvae **CONSTRUCT JEWELRY FROM GEMSTONES** and bits of precious metals.

CADDISFLY
ORDER TRICHOPTERA

Caddisflies make up an order of insects with more than 16,000 species. They are closely related to butterflies and moths, having two pairs of thin wings. But unlike those of butterflies and moths, their wings are hairy instead of scaly. Most larvae live in fresh water, but a few species are marine, meaning they live in the sea. One remarkable species from New Zealand and southern Australia (*Philanisus plebeius*) starts its life inside a cushion star (a type of sea star). How did it get there? The mother caddisfly has a long ovipositor for laying her eggs. During low tide, she flies up and down the coastline, and, when sea stars are exposed to the air, lays her eggs inside them.

After about one month, the larva hatches and makes its way out of the sea star. It then lives in tide pools, feeding on red algae. It makes a tubelike silk case to surround its body, which it often camouflages with bits of algae. It pokes its head out of its case to feed and move. After several larval molts, it turns into a pupa on the red algae. Eventually, an adult will emerge and fly free.

FACTS

OTHER COMMON NAME Sedge fly

SCIENTIFIC NAME Order: Trichoptera

SIZE 0.06–1.6 inches (1.5–40 mm)

WINGS Yes

FOOD Adult: most do not feed / Larva: small insects, leaves, and algae

HABITAT Near streams, ponds, and other bodies of water. Larvae live in water.

RANGE Worldwide except Antarctica

A freshwater caddisfly pupa in its case, which is **CAMOUFLAGED WITH STONES**

MORPHO
FAMILY NYMPHALIDAE

There's nothing like seeing a huge metallic-blue butterfly dancing across the rainforest canopy. You can find 30 morpho species in the tropical areas of Central and South America and Mexico. Many of them have iridescent blue on the top side of their wings. This may help other morphos to identify their own kind. But when a morpho comes to rest on the forest floor, it seems to disappear. That's because it closes its wings so only the lower sides of them are visible. The lower side is camouflaged with a mottled brown coloration. Morphos also have eye-spots on their wings that may deceive predators such as insect-eating birds, lizards, and frogs.

Males form territories and patrol along streams and rivers during the late morning. They chase away rivals. In many species, only the male is brightly colored. The female is duller.

FACTS

COMMON NAME Morpho

SCIENTIFIC NAME *Morpho* / Family: Nymphalidae

SIZE Wingspan of 3–8 inches (76–200 mm)

WINGS Yes

FOOD Adult: rotting fruit on the forest floor and sap / Larva: grasses, legumes, and other plants depending on species

HABITAT Primary rainforest and other woodlands

RANGE Tropical Central and South America and Mexico

Morphos don't drink nectar from flowers, **BUT FEED ON JUICES FROM ROTTING FRUIT AND ON SAP** flowing from wounds on trees and vines.

VICEROY BUTTERFLY
That's Fact-tastic!
Several other butterfly species MIMIC THE MONARCH'S ORANGE-AND-BLACK COLORATION, including viceroys, queens, and soldiers.

MONARCH BUTTERFLY

FAMILY NYMPHALIDAE

Monarch butterflies are famous for their yearly migrations that span several generations. In the fall, some of them fly up to 3,000 miles (4,800 km), from Canada to Mexico. The generation that emerges as adults in the fall isn't able to reproduce until after it completes its migration and regains its strength. Then it takes about three or four generations in spring and summer to complete the northward journey.

Imagine: The butterflies that make the long migration south to Mexico will follow the same path as generations before them, even though they have never made the journey before. (See the migration map on pages 50–51.)

The adults feed on nectar and lay eggs on milkweed plants. Monarch caterpillars bite the main vein of the milkweed leaf in order to stop the flow of the sticky, milky sap while they eat. They gain their toxicity from chemicals in the milkweed leaves. They retain that defense as pupae and adults. The bright orange and black wing colors of the adults serve as warning signs to predatory birds.

FACTS

COMMON NAME Monarch

SCIENTIFIC NAME *Danaus plexippus* / Family: Nymphalidae

SIZE Wingspan of 3.5–4 inches (89–102 mm)

WINGS Yes

FOOD Adult: nectar / Larva: milkweed plants (*Asclepias*)

HABITAT Meadows, gardens, and woodlands near host plants and nectar plants

RANGE Originally North, Central, and South America. Currently found in many countries.

POSTMAN
FAMILY NYMPHALIDAE

The postman and its relatives are remarkable and unique butterflies for so many reasons. They sleep in groups among twigs and tendrils and tend to return each night to the same place. They feed on pollen in addition to nectar. The protein-rich pollen helps them to live long lives for an insect (up to a year) and to lay eggs throughout their lifetime. Also, they have flashy colors to warn predators that they are toxic. And they fly slowly as if to advertise their distastefulness.

The postman gets its toxicity from its host plants—passion vines—which are laced with the poison cyanide. The larvae break down the poison and re-form it into their own nasty chemicals. The postman shares its color pattern with a number of other butterflies and moths. That pattern warns birds not to eat them.

OTHER COMMON NAME Common postman

SCIENTIFIC NAME *Heliconius melpomene* / Family: Nymphalidae

SIZE Wingspan of 2.17–3.15 inches (50–80 mm)

WINGS Yes

FOOD Adult: nectar and pollen / Larva: certain species of passion flower vines (*Passiflora*)

HABITAT Rainforest

RANGE Central and northern South America

Young birds that feed on butterflies must learn from experience what they can or can't eat. **DISTASTEFUL BUTTERFLIES LIKE THE POSTMAN SOMETIMES FLY AROUND WITH BATTLE SCARS FROM BIRDS—**beak-shaped bite marks on their wings. The butterflies are sometimes **ABLE TO ESCAPE.**

That's
Fact-tastic!

When the butterfly
emerges from its pupal case, it
NO LONGER HAS THE CHEMICAL
PROTECTION it did as a caterpillar.
But it's covered in lots of loose
scales that drop off as the
BUTTERFLY ESCAPES THE ANT
NEST. The loose scales help
to confuse the normally
aggressive ants.

ALCON BLUE
FAMILY LYCAENIDAE

The alcon blue butterfly has an amazing story to tell: It's raised by ants.

Life for the alcon blue begins as a tiny white egg. After a few days, the caterpillar hatches and feeds on its host plant for about two weeks. Then it drops to the ground and waits to be discovered by aggressive *Myrmica* ants. Fooled by the smell of chemicals the caterpillar secretes, the ants passing by will mistake the caterpillar for one of their own and carry it back to their underground nest. There, worker ants will feed the caterpillar regurgitated liquids from their mouths (photo below). The caterpillar also feeds the ants sugary droplets secreted from a gland on its back. The relationship between the ants and caterpillars, however, is not always mutually beneficial. The caterpillar also eats the ants' young—without the adult ants objecting! This makes the alcon blue a nest parasite on the *Myrmica* ants. It pupates inside the ant nest, and once the adult emerges, it must quickly flee the nest—or be attacked. Then it begins this remarkable cycle all over again.

FACTS

COMMON NAME Alcon blue

SCIENTIFIC NAME *Phengaris alcon* / Family: Lycaenidae

SIZE Wingspan of about 1.38 inches (35 mm)

WINGS Yes

FOOD Adult: nectar / Larva: marsh gentian and willow gentian host plants, then regurgitated liquids from worker ants, and ant larvae and pupae

HABITAT Where host plants and *Myrmica* ants live in the same place

RANGE Most of Europe and northern Asia

DEAD LEAF BUTTERFLY

FAMILY NYMPHALIDAE

In flight, the dead leaf butterfly is spectacular with its iridescent blue, orange, and black markings. But when it perches, it just plain disappears. With its wings closed, it's the spitting image of a dead leaf—right down to its veins. That's why it's called the dead leaf butterfly. The butterfly even flies so that it looks like a falling leaf. When it lands on the ground, it lies sideways and blends in with leaf litter.

Unlike most butterflies that are very similar in appearance among members of a species, the dead leaf varies a lot in the colors and pattern of dark splotches on the underside of its wings—even among siblings. For this reason, predatory birds can't memorize a particular "look," and this adds to the butterfly's incredible ability to blend in and hide.

FACTS

OTHER COMMON NAMES Orange oakleaf butterfly, Indian leaf butterfly

SCIENTIFIC NAME *Kallima inachus* / Family: Nymphalidae

SIZE 3.35–4.33 inches (85–110 mm)

WINGS Yes

FOOD Adult: rotting fruit on the forest floor / Larva: leaves of plants in the knotweed family and a few others

HABITAT Tropical forests

RANGE Tropical parts of Asia from India to Japan

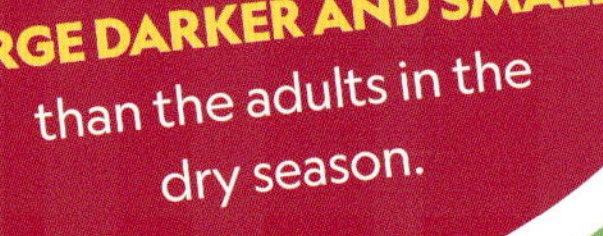

The dead leaf butterfly has **TWO GENERATIONS EACH YEAR,** one in the wet season and one in the dry season. (That means the first ones to lay eggs for the year will produce not just "children," but also "grandchildren" later that year.) The **ADULTS IN THE WET SEASON EMERGE DARKER AND SMALLER** than the adults in the dry season.

That's Fact-tastic!

When the female spicebush swallowtail is READY TO LAY EGGS, she flies around checking out potential host plants. She USES HER FRONT LEGS TO DRUM ON THE SURFACE OF DIFFERENT LEAVES. By doing this, she can taste if the plant is appropriate for her offspring. If so, she'll deposit her eggs on it.

SPICEBUSH SWALLOWTAIL
FAMILY PAPILIONIDAE

Adult spicebush swallowtails are dark butterflies that fly low in wooded areas. They flutter while visiting flowers like jewelweed and joe-pye weed. Sometimes they sip mineral-rich water from streams and wet soil. They readily group together with other species of butterflies when coming to puddles to drink. This is known as puddling. They also seek out mates and host plants to lay their eggs. Despite the fact that the adults are able to feed, they only tend to live between two days and two weeks.

To stay safe from predators, the larvae have several survival tricks. The caterpillars use silk to roll up part of a leaf, forming a shelter where they can't be seen by predators during the day. They come out to feed at night. The smallest caterpillars mimic bird droppings in their appearance. The larger ones have eyespots on their back (photo on right). When disturbed, they tuck their head under their body, puff up their front end, and flash the big false "eyes" to scare off birds and other predators. They can also release a foul odor when disturbed.

FACTS

COMMON NAME Spicebush swallowtail

SCIENTIFIC NAME *Papilio troilus* / Family: Papilionidae

SIZE Wingspan of about 3.5–4.5 inches (89–114 mm)

WINGS Yes

FOOD Adult: nectar and mineral-rich water / Larva: spicebush, sassafras, and redbay

HABITAT Shady areas, especially in woodlands and woody swampland

RANGE Eastern United States and southern Ontario, Canada

APOLLO BUTTERFLY
FAMILY PAPILIONIDAE

This gorgeous butterfly is highly prized by butterfly watchers and collectors. During the summer, it can be seen in flowery meadows in the Alps and other mountainous habitats in Europe. But it has been declining in numbers and disappearing from parts of its former range.

The apollo requires open meadows with nectar-producing flowers next to rocky outcrops, where they find their host plants. The female lays her eggs on the host, and the following spring the caterpillars hatch out and eat the host's leaves. If one habitat, for example the meadow, is altered or destroyed, then the rocky outcrops aren't sufficient for the apollo butterfly to survive.

The apollo's habitat is gradually being replaced by agriculture, tree plantations, and buildings. Other serious problems in different locations include over-collecting and accidents with cars. Climate change may also be playing a role in the butterfly's declining population. Now there are laws in various countries to protect the apollo. Conservationists are focusing their efforts on protecting the apollo's habitats and on raising and releasing butterflies into their natural environment.

FACTS

OTHER COMMON NAME Mountain apollo

SCIENTIFIC NAME *Parnassius apollo* / Family: Papilionidae

SIZE Wingspan of about 2.75–3.5 inches (70–90 mm) / Females are larger than males

WINGS Yes

FOOD Adult: nectar / Larva: stonecrop *(Sedum)* and houseleeks *(Sempervivum)*

HABITAT Mountain meadows and pastures, and rocky outcrops

RANGE Europe and Central Asia

That's Fact-tastic!

Individual butterflies of the same species tend to look alike. But some, like the apollo, have **A LOT OF VARIATION AMONG THEMSELVES—**such as in the number, size, and color of their spots.

COMMON JEZEBEL BUTTERFLY

FAMILY PIERIDAE

The jezebel flies high in the forest canopy, feeding on flower nectar. This species is dull on the upper side of the wings, but its underside explodes with bright colors—yellow, orange-red, black, and white. The bright colors advertise the jezebel's toxicity, which it gets from feeding on mistletoe plants as a caterpillar. When predatory birds see the colors, they know to avoid these butterflies.

Young caterpillars feed in dense clusters. When disturbed, they bungee jump from a silk thread formed by the silk gland on the underside of the head. They climb back up the thread when the coast is clear.

FACTS

COMMON NAME Common jezebel

SCIENTIFIC NAME *Delias eucharis* / Family: Pieridae

SIZE Wingspan of 2.5–3.35 inches (65–85 mm)

WINGS Yes

FOOD Adult: nectar / Larva: mistletoe (*Loranthus*)

HABITAT Almost anywhere with trees, including gardens

RANGE Wetter regions of India, Sri Lanka, Myanmar, and Thailand

Butterflies in the family Pieridae can look very different from each other. These are green pierid butterflies gathered by a riverbank in Bolivia. The males of many pierid butterflies, including the common jezebel, **EXHIBIT MUD-PUDDLING BEHAVIOR.** They gather together and **DRINK MINERAL SALTS FROM PUDDLES** and moist soils.

BUTTERFLIES GALLERY

Butterflies have amazing wings made up of thousands of tiny scales. These scales can be brightly colored or dull, and even transparent. Some butterflies have shiny, metallic colors, like the morpho.

Butterflies use their wing colors and patterns in many ways. They can be used for camouflage, to absorb heat, and to find a mate. Some toxic butterflies also rely on their bright colors to warn predators that they taste foul. Potential enemies, like birds, learn to keep away. With about 20,000 butterfly species, these fluttering insects live just about anywhere in the world. They can be found in rainforests, mountaintops, deserts, cities, and even your own backyard. Do you have a favorite of the species shown here?

A small skipper butterfly rests at attention on a flower stalk. Skippers have strong wing muscles for darting in flight.

The Cairns birdwing is Australia's largest native butterfly. It inhabits the rainforests of Queensland on the northeast coast.

The peacock butterfly lives in Europe and parts of Asia. Its flashy eye-spots may help deter predation. Adult butterflies hibernate over the winter.

A Malayan zebra butterfly drinks from moist, rocky soil. In Southeast Asia, these butterflies are often seen mud-puddling with other butterflies.

A close-up of a butterfly's iridescent wing scales. The optically formed colors that you see depend on the angle at which you look at the wings.

This cattleheart butterfly is a type of swallowtail butterfly. Its fuzzy thorax is covered in tightly packed black and red hairs.

That's Fact-tastic!

IN CHINA the name of the atlas moth TRANSLATES TO "SNAKE'S HEAD," because of the extensions on the TIPS OF THEIR FOREWINGS, which strongly RESEMBLE A SNAKE'S HEAD.

ATLAS MOTH

FAMILY SATURNIIDAE

The atlas moth is one of the largest moths in the world. Its wingspan is almost one foot (30 cm) wide and the surface area of its wings is about 62 square inches (400 sq cm). That's about the size of this page turned sideways.

These spectacular moths are hard to find in the wild. For one thing, they fly at night. Also, the adults have no proboscis for feeding, so they don't live long. They might last a week or two off their fat reserves. That means they have limited time to mate and lay eggs. The male can fly a couple of miles or more, using his feathery antennae to pursue a female's powerful, airborne pheromone (scent) trail.

The atlas moth is in the silk moth family. The caterpillars make a cocoon with very strong silk threads (see page 48). In Taiwan, empty cocoons are used as small change purses.

FACTS

COMMON NAME Atlas moth

SCIENTIFIC NAME *Attacus atlas* / Family: Saturniidae

SIZE Wingspan sometimes more than 10 inches (250 mm)

WINGS Yes

FOOD Adult: does not eat / Larva: leaves of certain citrus and other evergreen trees

HABITAT Tropical and subtropical forests and shrublands

RANGE India to Southeast Asia and Australia

LOBSTER MOTH

FAMILY NOTODONTIDAE

The caterpillars of the lobster moth are bizarre-looking, and they change their appearance as they grow. When a caterpillar hatches from its egg, it feeds on its eggshell and looks like an ant or spider with spindly legs. It even moves like an ant. It guards its eggshell and viciously attacks intruders. After the first molt, it switches to feeding on leaves of its host plants. With each successive molt, it develops an unusual-shaped body with a large head and tail end—eventually looking much like a lobster. It has two attachments on the end of its abdomen that are really caterpillar legs. When the caterpillar is disturbed by predators, it reaches out with its long front legs and throws its head back in a menacing display.

The caterpillar makes a strong cocoon and transforms into a pupa where it stays for the winter. It emerges as a brown, furry-looking adult in the spring.

FACTS

OTHER COMMON NAME Lobster prominent

SCIENTIFIC NAME *Stauropus fagi* / Family: Notodontidae

SIZE Wingspan of 1.6–2.75 inches (40–70 mm)

WINGS Yes

FOOD Adult: may not feed / Larva: leaves of oak, beech, birch trees, or hazel

HABITAT Woodlands

RANGE Europe and northern parts of Asia, up to the Arctic

AN ADULT lobster moth

The lobster moth belongs to a family that has some bizarre-looking caterpillars with humps, bumps, and spines. When they're not feeding, they often rest with their front and back ends raised.

BOGONG MOTH

FAMILY NOCTUIDAE

Bogong moths can't stand the heat. Each spring, when the temperature begins to rise, the moths leave their home in the wheat-growing areas of Queensland, Australia. They head south for the Australian Alps, where the climate is cool. They can journey more than 620 miles (1,000 km) on their migration.

The moths travel in huge numbers, and they make pit stops on rocks, buildings, and trees. At rest, their wings overlap like a tiled roof. Bogongs fly at night and unfortunately are attracted to city lights that take them off course. In recent years many haven't reached their destination in the mountains where they normally sleep through the summer in cool caves and crevices. The light pollution has been so bad that people are asked to turn off their outdoor lights for two months during the moths' peak migration. When Bogong moths don't reach the southern mountains, other animals like the critically endangered mountain pygmy possum can suffer for lack of food.

FACTS

COMMON NAME Bogong moth

SCIENTIFIC NAME *Agrotis infusa* / Family: Noctuidae

SIZE Wingspan of about 1.6–2 inches (40–50 mm)

WINGS Yes

FOOD Adult: nectar / Larva: grasses and forbs, including crop plants

HABITAT Changes over the year with their migrations

RANGE Southern Australia

That's Fact-tastic!

MOUNTAIN PYGMY POSSUMS hibernate over winter. When summer comes, they **FEED ON BOGONG MOTHS,** along with other insects, fruits, and seeds.

WALLACE'S SPHINX MOTH

FAMILY SPHINGIDAE

Wallace's sphinx moth has the longest proboscis of any moth—up to 14 inches (355 mm) long. Its proboscis is three times longer than its body!

The famous naturalist Charles Darwin never got to see this moth, but he predicted its existence. He received a package of star orchids from Madagascar that startled him. Each flower had a nectar spur that was extremely long—up to 14 inches. Darwin wrote that in order for an insect to drink nectar from it, it would need an equally long proboscis. He predicted that a moth of that description would be the pollinator. As it drank nectar it would get pollen rubbed onto its head, then the moth would pollinate other flowers it visited. Five years after Darwin's prediction, another famous naturalist, Alfred Russell Wallace, likewise predicted the existence of the moth.

Both Darwin and Wallace got it right. The newly named Wallace's sphinx moth was the mystery pollinator. It plunges its super long proboscis into the orchid's nectar spur, hovering like a hummingbird while it drinks. Then the moth transfers pollen to other star orchid flowers.

COMMON NAME Wallace's sphinx moth

SCIENTIFIC NAME *Xanthopan praedicta* / Family: Sphingidae

SIZE Wingspan of 5–6 inches (130–150 mm) / Proboscis up to 14 inches (355 mm)

WINGS Yes

FOOD Adult: nectar from *Angraecum sesquipedale* / Larva: leaves of wild custard-apple, soursop, and a few other plants

HABITAT Rainforest in eastern Madagascar

RANGE Madagascar

There are **ABOUT 1,450 SPECIES OF SPHINX MOTHS.** They hover when they visit flowers for nectar.

MADAGASCAN SUNSET MOTH

FAMILY URANIIDAE

It's easy to think the Madagascan sunset moth is a butterfly. The wings have tails like a swallowtail butterfly, and it's so colorful. But the beautiful iridescence of its wings is an optical illusion. The color shifts as you look at it from different angles.

The females lay their eggs on toxic tropical host plants of the genus *Omphalea*. The toxins don't hurt the caterpillar, but help it to avoid predators throughout its life. The host plants live mainly near the east and west coasts of Madagascar. When the western host plants are hit by drought, the moths migrate to *Omphalea* trees in eastern Madagascar in order to survive. (See the section on migration on pages 50–51.)

Not all moths in this family are day fliers like the Madagascan sunset moth. The ones that fly by day tend to have bright colors, but the ones that fly at night tend to be drab.

FACTS

COMMON NAME Madagascan sunset moth

SCIENTIFIC NAME *Chrysiridia rhipheus* / Family: Uraniidae

SIZE Wingspan of 2.75–3.5 inches (70–90 mm)

WINGS Yes

FOOD Adult: nectar / Larva: *Omphalea* leaves

HABITAT Dry areas on the west coast and rainforest on the east coast

RANGE Madagascar

That's Fact-tastic!

During the **VICTORIAN ERA** (1837–1901), people made jewelry out of the wings of the **MADAGASCAN SUNSET MOTH.**

EASTERN TENT CATERPILLAR MOTH

FAMILY LASIOCAMPIDAE

Eastern tent caterpillars hatch from a mass of eggs in the early spring. A single group may include about 300 caterpillars!

After hatching, the caterpillars work together to make a silk tent in the tree branches where they live. The broad side of the tent faces the sun and helps to keep the caterpillars warm on cold days. As they grow, they add more layers of silk to enlarge the tent. Caterpillars often huddle inside; they may also sit on the outside to bask in the sun. When they're hungry, they leave their tent and "follow the leader" out to the branch tips to eat the leaves. If ants, birds, or other predators should disturb them, they rear up and thrash back and forth—all in unison! Their bodies are covered in bristles that can irritate predators. They can also retreat to the safety of their tent.

The adult
eastern tent
moth with its
wings closed

A group of eastern tent
caterpillars on their silk
tent. A few can be seen
inside it.

TEAR-DRINKING MOTH

FAMILY NOLIDAE

Tear-drinking moths have a very special diet. They feed on tears—mainly of zebus and other large hoofed mammals.

Zebus are a common type of cattle in several south-east Asian countries. At night, tear-drinking moths fly to a zebu and line up around the rim of its eyes. They stick their proboscis into the animal's eye to drink up its tears. Tears are made up of water, salts, and some protein—enough to sustain small moths. If the zebu doesn't have moist eyes, no problem—the moth sweeps its spine-tipped proboscis across the eyeball to irritate it so that it makes more tears. If the zebu is sleeping with closed eyes, still no problem—the moth plunges its proboscis between the closed lids.

There are just over 100 known species of moths from several different families that specialize in drinking tears. One that feeds on elephant tears in Thailand is aptly named the elephant-tear moth.

FACTS

OTHER COMMON NAMES Tear-feeding moth, eye-frequenting moth

SCIENTIFIC NAME *Lobocraspis griseifusa* / Family: Nolidae

SIZE 1.4–1.5 inches (35–38 mm)

WINGS Yes

FOOD Adult: tears / Larva: plants

HABITAT Near livestock

RANGE Myanmar, Thailand, and Cambodia

Like tear-drinking moths, the **VAMPIRE MOTH** (*Calyptra eustrigata*) has a very specialized diet: **IT DRINKS BLOOD FROM MAMMALS, INCLUDING PEOPLE.** But unlike blood-drinking female mosquitoes, **ONLY THE MALE VAMPIRE MOTHS DRINK BLOOD.** In the photo to the right, the vampire moth is drinking blood from the furry back of a tapir.

CATERPILLARS GALLERY

The larvae of butterflies and moths display a tremendous amount of diversity in form, diet, and behavior. Their defenses against predators like birds, lizards, and monkeys are remarkable. Some have spines, false eyes, toxic bodies, or warning coloration, and a few tiny moth larvae even live on the inside of leaves, tunneling through them as they eat and grow. Some other species can escape danger by reeling out a silk thread. They dangle from it until they feel safe to return. Many caterpillars feed on the underside of leaves where birds can't easily see them. A few even roll themselves up in a leaf and stitch the leaf shut with their silk. Hiding out during the daytime and coming out at night to feed is a survival strategy used by many caterpillars. Plus, there are lots and lots of chemical defenses that different species of caterpillars rely on to stay alive. Here's a small sample of the many caterpillars found in nature.

A venomous monkey slug caterpillar resembles a hairy spider. If attacked, it can detach its false legs and grow them back at the next molt.

This jelly slug caterpillar's body is protected by a translucent gelatin that it secretes from glands on its back.

A well-fattened mangrove skipper caterpillar in its final stage before becoming a pupa. It has two bright orange eyespots on its head.

A cecropia moth caterpillar tucks its head down and displays its colorful, spiny knobs (called tubercles).

A large Pluto sphinx moth caterpillar has false eyes and a tail. The real eyes are located on its head, which is tucked under.

A spotted apatelodes caterpillar looks soft and cuddly, but it has some hidden toxin-filled spines that deliver a painful sting.

SPIDERS

SOUTHERN BLACK WIDOW SPIDER
A GREENBOTTLE BLUE TARANTULA WALKING ACROSS MOSS
DADDY LONGLEGS SPIDER, ALSO CALLED A CELLAR SPIDER
A PINK-AND-WHITE CRAB SPIDER POISED TO AMBUSH AN UNSUSPECTING INSECT
A HAWAIIAN HAPPY-FACE SPIDER GUARDING HER EGGS

ONE OF INSECTS' CLOSEST RELATIVES

Spiders may seem like insects, but they're actually arachnids—a class of invertebrate animals that includes scorpions, ticks, and mites. Unlike insects, which have three body parts, arachnids have only two: the cephalothorax (head and thorax combined) and the abdomen. They have eight legs, while insects have six. Also, arachnids lack the wings, antennae, and compound eyes that insects have. Instead, they have simple eyes—many species having eight, but some having six, four, two, or no eyes. Spiders, like insects, can be found almost anywhere in the world, except for Antarctica.

All spiders are strictly meat-eating carnivores with the exception of one from Central America that also eats plants. Spiders eat insects, such as moths, crickets, and flies. Some species even eat larger animals such as birds and frogs.

Once they catch a meal, spiders must immobilize their prey. Many spiders inject venom from their fangs to paralyze it. Some, especially ones with short fangs, wrap their prey tightly in silk first before injecting it.

When it's time to eat, spiders either inject digestive juices into their prey with their fangs or secrete the juices from their jaws. The digestive juices break down the prey's tissues. When the tissues become a liquid, the spider slurps it up. Some larger spiders, such as tarantulas, also have prominent teeth for tearing and grinding up their prey.

Spiders deserve our respect. They control insect populations and, in turn, become food for birds and many other animals. Although most spiders aren't harmful to us, a few species deliver a bite that can be painful or even deadly. And for that reason, it's best to look but not touch. There are almost 55,000 spider species. Check out a few of them here and on the next two gallery pages.

SCIENTIFIC CLASSIFICATION OF A SPIDER
Kingdom: Animalia (animals)
Phylum: Arthropoda (jointed legs; or more precisely, "jointed foot")
Class: Arachnida (spiders and relatives)
Order: Araneae
Family: Pisauridae (nursery web spiders)
Genus: Pisaura
Species: Pisaura mirabilis
SPINNERETS
ABDOMEN
CEPHALOTHORAX
The way a spider's EYES ARE ARRANGED on its head is KEY TO IDENTIFYING THE FAMILY in which it belongs.
EIGHT EYES
MANDIBLES
FANGS

SPIDERS GALLERY

The ant-mimicking jumping spider looks and acts like an ant.

This spider is releasing silk as it lofts itself into the air.

A wolf spider with a fly in its huge jaws. Wolf spiders are members of the family Lycosidae.

A goldenrod crab spider is visible against purple flowers, but on goldenrod plants, it's hard to find.

This raft spider caught a stickleback fish for a meal.

A male peacock spider dances to attract a mate.

This leggy huntsman spider doesn't build webs; instead it relies on its incredible speed to catch prey.

SPIDERWEBS GALLERY

As a group, spiders excel in their hunting strategies. To catch their prey, different kinds of spiders specialize in different methods. Some hunt down and grab their victim. Others hide out and ambush it. About one-third of known spiders make webs. Web-making spiders construct all kinds of structures to help them catch a meal, such as orbs, funnels, and sheets.

Spider silk is super strong. One thread of silk is stronger than a thread of steel of the same thickness! The silk starts out as a liquid inside glands in the spider's abdomen. As it is drawn out of tiny openings in the spinnerets, it becomes threadlike. Some spiders add a sticky glue to the threads to prevent prey from escaping the web. Check out these super spiderwebs.

The European water spider attaches its web to underwater plants, then traps a big air bubble on the underside. These spiders breathe, eat, rest, and mate inside the bubble. To replenish the air, they swim to the surface, where air sticks to their hairy bodies. Then they bring the air back to the bubble.

Many spiders make orb webs. Orb weavers might construct their webs with up to seven different kinds of silk. Some orb weaver silk is sticky and stretchy; some is super strong. Orb webs can be hard to see but easily trap flying insects.

Silk threads radiate from the funnel-web spider's burrow. Passing prey jiggle the web and alert the spider, whose venom is very toxic. The spider pounces on its prey and bites, injecting the fatal venom.

The net-casting spider, also known as the ogre-faced spider, is a nocturnal arachnid. It starts its web by attaching silk threads to branches from which it can hang. Then it makes a big netlike web that it holds in its front legs and casts out over its prey.

Trapdoor spiders make a silk-lined underground burrow with a hinged lid. Silk threads spread across the ground and pick up the vibration of passing prey. When the spider feels a vibration, it jumps from its burrow, grabs its prey, and returns underground, closing the lid.

This argiope spider weaves a zigzag pattern in its orb web. The decoration reflects UV light that attracts prey. The patterns on the spider's body blend in a bit with the web decoration, making it harder for an insect to spot it.

A COLORADO POTATO BEETLE LARVA ON A POTATO LEAF

AN ADULT TWO-LINED SPITTLEBUG IN A FROTHY MASS

AN ARGIOPE SPIDER IN ITS WEB

A PUSS MOTH CATERPILLAR IN A DEFENSIVE POSTURE

RED-BANDED LEAFHOPPER

MORE ABOUT BUGS

A TALK WITH ENTOMOLOGIST BILL LAMP

Entomologists are scientists who study insects and arachnids. There are many different types of entomologists. Some research the adaptations and habitats of certain insects to learn more about them. And some identify ways to help conserve insects that are endangered.

Bill Lamp is an entomologist at the University of Maryland in College Park, Maryland. We spoke to Bill to learn more about what entomologists like him do, and to get some bug-studying tips.

Potato leafhoppers are insects that migrate to areas where food is abundant. They feed on the leaves of many different crops, such as potato, alfalfa, clover, soybean, strawberry, and eggplant. The leafhoppers use a sharp mouthpart called a stylet to pierce the plants, and they produce saliva as they feed. Together, these two factors cause the leaves to brown. The effect is sometimes called "hopperburn."

What do entomologists do?

The range of study by entomologists is vast. Just to give a few examples, some of us study pollination of flowers by insects. Others study medically important insects, such as malaria-bearing mosquitoes, while others discover new species of insects around the globe. And still others specialize in pest management.

Tell us more about what you do.

I have a diverse research program that includes both aquatic insects and insects that feed on plants. My students and I have published papers on mayflies, caddisflies, and aquatic beetles from streams and wetlands. My major focus has been on sap-feeding insects such as leafhoppers and stink bugs, because of their ability to injure agriculturally important plants.

What inspired you to become an entomologist?

During college, I signed up to take an aquatic entomology course at the Lake Itasca Biology Station in Minnesota. On our first day, our professor took us to the headwaters of the Mississippi River. We collected insects from the stream, under stones, on branches, and along the edges. I was fascinated by all that I saw and later learned about aquatic insects.

How is climate change affecting insects?

Climate change is one of many global environmental factors that affect insect species. Insects are ectotherms, with body temperatures similar to that of their surroundings. When it's too hot or too cold, growing, walking, flying, and reproducing slow down. Other extreme weather conditions, such as drought or excessive rain, can harm insects. Even the lack of snow cover can make soil too cold to survive. As insects slowly relocate to more favorable habitats, the distribution of plants, birds, and other animals also changes. To protect local insect populations, grow native plants and trees, reduce harmful chemicals, and learn all you can!

What advice would you give kids who want to study insects?

The easiest way to collect insects to temporarily study them is with a simple sweep net—you just sweep up some grass or plants and then place the contents into a jar or cage, or even a sealable plastic bag. Then take a look to see if there are any insects inside. Once you spot them, release them and watch them carefully in nature to see what they might be doing.

When you get up close to an insect, what do you look at or for?

Observing the wings is good, like their number, size, and texture, because they are often used for identification. For example, a stinging bee has four wings, but a fly that mimics the bee and pretends to sting only has two.

How much time do you spend studying a particular insect?

I have studied the potato leafhopper, *Empoasca fabae*, since 1980—over 40 years! Other insects I've studied are stink bugs, aquatic beetles, mayflies, and caddisflies.

Have you ever discovered an insect?

I did discover a fly that was new to North America. I was identifying insects that feed on thistle plants, and I raised the adult fly from larvae that fed on the roots of the thistle. A fly expert at the United States Department of Agriculture (USDA) identified the fly for me as a species that came from Europe.

What tips can you offer for kids who want to observe insects in their backyard or at a nearby park or pond?

There are hundreds of species of insects that occur in a backyard over the course of a year. I would recommend that you keep your eyes open for any opportunity to find insects. Many are attracted to lights, so around porch lights is a great place. Insects like moist, dark places, so under fallen logs is a good place too. If you take a careful look at plants, the soil surface, flowers, or along streams and ponds, you will likely find insects there as well.

How should kids handle insects they observe?

It's okay to keep an insect for a short period of time if you're planning to observe certain behaviors, such as feeding and adult emergence. But be careful! Insects are easily injured by handling. Be aware that some insects sting or bite. You can tell by their [bright] coloration that they're dangerous. So keep a safe distance during this time. After you're done with your observation, release them back into the environment.

HOW YOU CAN HELP

With thousands of insect species facing the possibility of extinction in our lifetime, people need to find ways to solve the big problems. What can you do to help? Here are some ideas.

CREATE A BUTTERFLY GARDEN

Create a safe haven for butterflies by encouraging your family or school to plant a butterfly garden. What can you include in your garden? Brightly colored and strong-scented flowers, such as butterfly weed, lantana, and zinnias. These flowers not only attract butterflies, but they also contain nectar, which is an important food source. You'll also want to stock your garden with host plants where butterflies can lay their eggs. Some examples of host plants are milkweed, willow, and fennel. Check out the National Geographic Kids website for information on how to create a butterfly garden.

PLANT A BEE GARDEN

Bees need nectar and pollen from plants to survive. But with land development increasing, there are fewer places where bees can find the right plants. You can help by encouraging your family and friends to plant a bee garden. To get started, go to your local gardening store for plants that bees prefer, such as daisies, sunflowers, mint, and marigolds. These flowers produce lots of nectar. If you plant different types of seeds that grow in different seasons, your garden will bloom for most of the year. After planting, avoid using fertilizers and pesticides, which can harm bees.

REDUCE WATER POLLUTION

As you've seen in this book, various insects spend all or part of their life in water. This includes, dragonflies, damselflies, water bugs, water striders, mayflies, caddisflies, and even certain spiders. These creatures make up a healthy wetland environment. But here's the conundrum—we want to promote healthy wetlands, but not encourage the growth of potentially harmful mosquitoes. Using pesticides to kill mosquitoes can also kill the many harmless insects that make up a healthy wetland.

So, how can you help? For one, don't create places to breed mosquitoes by letting water stand for days in containers such as buckets, birdbaths, tarps, dog bowls, kiddie pools, and plant saucers. Dump the standing water or change the water at least once a week.

If it's necessary to remove mosquitoes by another method, you can have an adult use a Bti product. Bti is a bacterium that kills mosquito larvae without affecting other organisms.

USE COMPOST

Some fertilizers contain pesticides and other chemicals that can be harmful to insects and other wildlife. Encourage your family to ditch these harmful products in favor of compost. Compost is rotting organic matter, like grass clippings, leaves, and leftover food scraps such as apple cores, eggshells, and bread crumbs. When this rotting matter is mixed with soil, organisms such as beetles, bacteria, fungi, and other organisms will break down the compost. This releases nutrients into the soil and helps plants grow. And most important, compost is harmless to wildlife.

JOIN AN ORGANIZATION

Spreading the news about endangered insects raises public awareness about the matter. Educate yourself by joining a group like the Xerces Society, which publishes information about endangered insects and offers tips on how to help.

HELP CURB GLOBAL CLIMATE CHANGE

According to scientists, burning fossil fuels, like oil and gasoline, releases heat-trapping gases into the atmosphere. The result is global climate change. This phenomenon threatens insects in many ways. For example, it makes it difficult for plants, which some insects use as food and shelter, to grow. You can help reduce the burning of fossil fuels by turning off the lights when you leave a room and using energy-saving bulbs. Put on a sweater instead of turning up the heat, and towel dry your hair instead of blow-drying it.

PICK UP THE TRASH

Water pollution can make it hard for some water-dwelling insects to breathe and find food, while ground litter can make it difficult for trees and other plants—sources of shelter and food for many insects—to grow. So help keep your neighborhood, forests, and parks clean. Put on a pair of gloves to pick up trash and discourage "litter bugs" from doing further damage. If you can't discard larger items, such as tires and bins, be sure to empty them of any rainwater that collects inside. Reducing standing water, where mosquitoes breed, will help control their population.

GLOSSARY

ADAPTATION: a feature that helps a living organism survive in its environment

ALGAE: simple, plantlike organisms that lack true stems, roots, and leaves. Algae range in size from single-celled species to giant kelp. They can live in fresh water or salt water and in moist places on land.

AQUATIC INSECTS: insects that spend part or all of their life in fresh water

BIOLUMINESCENCE: the production of light by a living organism

CAMOUFLAGE: an organism's ability to disguise its appearance, often by using its coloring or body shape to blend in with its surroundings. An example is a stick insect that looks just like a stick.

CARCASS: the dead body of an animal

CARNIVORE: an organism that eats meat. For example, insects that eat other insects are carnivores.

CARRION: the decaying flesh of a dead animal

COLONY: a group of the same kind of organism living or growing together. In social insects, such as leafcutter ants, colonies are typically large extended families.

COMMON NAME: the nonscientific name of an organism that is used by a community of people. Not all common names are the same in all regions. For example, a "buff-tailed bumblebee" in one region may be known as a "large earth bumblebee" in another.

COMPOUND EYE: an eye found in insects and some crustaceans that is made up of many light-sensitive units called ommatidia. With few exceptions, these six-sided units are joined together in a honeycomb pattern. The ommatidia form separate images that are united in the brain to form one picture.

COURTSHIP: a behavior used by animals to attract each other for mating

DEFENSE: a means by which an organism protects itself from attack or harm. Defenses can be part of an animal's body (for example, its spines), part of its coloring, part of its chemistry (an insect may be able to squirt acid, for instance), or its behavior (it can hide).

DEFOLIATE: to remove leaves from a plant, such as when certain insects eat the leaves

EGG CASE: a capsule that contains eggs. In certain insects, the mother makes a silk case (or capsule) that surrounds her fertilized eggs and protects them until they hatch.

ELYTRA: the hardened forewings, or wing covers, of certain insects, especially beetles. The elytra protect the functioning hind wings.

ENDANGERED: relating to an animal or plant that is found in such small numbers that it is at risk of becoming extinct, or no longer existing

ENVIRONMENT: the natural features of a place, such as its weather, the kind of land it has, and the type of plants that grow in it

EXTINCTION: the state of no longer existing, or being alive. When all the members of a species die out, the species is said to go extinct.

EYESPOT: a round marking resembling an eye, such as a spot that appears on the wings of some butterflies. In some organisms, eyespots are a form of mimicry. An individual of a species will recognize other individuals of its species by their eyespots and other unique color patterns.

FOLIAGE: a cluster of leaves on a plant, tree, vine, or shrub. Also, the leaves of all plants in an area. An example of its use is in the term "fall foliage."

FORAGE: to search widely for food

FOREWINGS: the two front wings of a four-winged insect

FOSSIL: the preserved remains or traces of an organism that lived a long time ago

FUNGUS: an organism that produces spores and feeds on organic matter. Many species of fungi produce fruiting bodies called mushrooms, which release the spores when they mature.

GENERATION: all of the insects of a species that were hatched at about the same time. Some insects, especially social insects (like termites and ants), have overlapping generations, meaning that their young are continually being produced.

HABITAT: a place in nature where an organism lives throughout the year, or for shorter periods of time

HIND WINGS: the two back wings of a four-winged insect

HONEYDEW: a sweet, sticky substance that some insects, such as aphids and some bugs, secrete from their abdomens

HOST: an organism that a parasite feeds on. The parasite/host relationship is different from a predator/prey relationship. Typically, prey are killed and fed upon by a predator, whereas a host is somewhat hurt or disabled by its parasite. However, if a "host" is attacked by a parasitoid, it is fed on gradually, and eventually it dies.

HOST PLANT: a species of plant that an insect or other organism depends on, usually as a source of food. For example, milkweeds are the host plants for monarch butterfly caterpillars.

INSECT CLASSIFICATION: The grouping of insects based on their relatedness and their physical characteristics. For example, the class Insecta (insects) is divided into orders (such as Diptera, or flies). The order is divided into families. Each family is divided into genera (the plural of genus), and each genus is divided into species. (In some cases, there is only one member of a family or genus.) The species has a double name that is italicized. The first name is the genus name, followed by a specific name.

INVASIVE SPECIES: a species that is introduced accidentally or on purpose from its native habitat to a new location. Also called an "introduced species" or an "exotic species." Invasive species typically have a bad effect on native plants and animals.

INVERTEBRATE: an organism without a backbone. Invertebrates include insects, arachnids, crustaceans, and mollusks.

IRIDESCENT: displaying rainbowlike colors that change when seen from different angles. The wings of a Madagascan sunset moth are an example.

LARVA (plural: larvae): an immature form of an insect with complete metamorphosis. Larvae have alternative names such as caterpillars (for butterflies and moths), grubs (for beetles, bees, and wasps), maggots (for flies), and wrigglers (for mosquitoes). In the process of metamorphosis, the larva becomes the pupa, and then the adult.

LUCIFERASE: a particular enzyme (substance) produced in bioluminescent organisms, such as fireflies and glowworms, to make light

MANDIBLES: in insects, crustaceans, and centipedes, a pair of appendages, or jaws, used mainly for tearing and chewing food, and for carrying objects. Some insects, such as butterflies and most moths, lack mandibles as adults, but their larvae have them.

MEASUREMENT: the length, height, or width of something. In most areas of the world, the metric system is the preferred system of measurement, while in the United States, U.S. standard units are used. Some common units of measurement include:
1 millimeter (mm) = 0.04 inch (in)
1 centimeter (cm) = 0.4 inch (in)
1 meter (m) = 3.3 feet (ft)
1 kilometer (km) = 3,281 feet (ft)
1 gram (g) = 0.04 ounce (oz)
1 kilogram (kg) = 2.2 pounds (lb)

METAMORPHOSIS: in insects, it is the process of changing from an immature form to an adult form. Insects with simple metamorphosis go from egg to nymph to adult. Those with complete metamorphosis go from egg to larva to pupa to adult.

MIGRATION: in insects, the seasonal movement from one location to another. The migration may be prompted by various environmental cues, including weather and availability of food. Monarch butterflies and Bogong moths are examples of insects that migrate.

MIMICRY: the similarity of one species to another (or others) that can act to protect one or more species. The similarity might not be just in appearance, but also in sounds, smells, or behavior. Butterflies with nearly identical wing color patterns are often said to exhibit mimicry.

MOTTLED: covered with spots or having colored areas

MUD-PUDDLING: a behavior seen mostly in butterflies, in which they drink from wet soil to obtain moisture and nutrients. Butterflies can often be seen mud-puddling in groups.

NECTAR: a sweet liquid secreted by plants as food to attract animals that will benefit them. Many flowers produce nectar to attract pollinating insects, birds, and bats. Nectar consists primarily of water and sugars, including fructose, glucose, and sucrose.

NYMPH: the immature form of an insect with simple metamorphosis. The nymphs of flying insects have wing buds on their back, unlike larvae, which start to develop wings inside the pupa. Nymphs look like smaller versions of the adult, and often feed on the same type of food.

ORGANIC MATERIAL: matter that remains of dead plants and animals and their waste products

OVIPOSITOR: the egg-laying organ on a female insect and some other animals. In some insects, the ovipositor is also used to burrow into soil or plant tissues, or to pierce wood prior to laying eggs. Certain wasps, bees, and ants use their ovipositor as a stinger.

PARASITE: an insect (or any organism) that lives on or inside another species of organism (the host) and feeds on it. Generally, a parasite does not kill the host. But a form of parasite called a parasitoid grows up feeding on its live host, which eventually kills the host. Many types of organisms can be considered parasitoids, but of the insect parasitoids, the most common are certain wasps and flies.

PHEROMONE: an airborne chemical secreted by an insect (or other animal) that influences the behavior of other members of the same species. Certain pheromones can attract mates, others can be used to sound the alarm to nest-mates, and still others can be used to mark a trail to food sources. Pheromones are a form of chemical communication.

POLLEN: tiny grains produced by the male part of flowers that fertilize the future seeds of a plant of the same species. Many plants recruit insects (known as pollinators) to carry the pollen from one flower or plant to another in the process of pollination.

PREDATOR: an animal that hunts other animals for food. Its behavior is "predatory."

PREY: an animal that is hunted and eaten by other animals

PROBOSCIS: in insects, the elongated tubular mouthparts for drinking a liquid meal

PRONOTUM: a hardened plate on the top of the thorax just behind the head of insects. The pronotum is part of the insect's exoskeleton. Tree-hoppers, for example, have exceptionally large pronotums compared with the rest of their body.

PUPA (plural: pupae): a life stage of insects with complete metamorphosis during which the larval body is replaced with an adult body. Although the pupa is generally immobile, it undergoes tremendous changes on the inside. The pupa is enclosed in a cocoon in certain insects. Other names for insect pupae are chrysalises (in butterflies) and tumblers (in mosquitoes).

RAINFOREST: an evergreen forest with upwards of 160 inches (406 cm) of rain in a year. There are both tropical and temperate rainforests.

SCAVENGER: an animal (insect) that feeds on dead or decaying matter.

SCIENTIFIC NAME: a unique two-part name used by scientists to identify each type of organism. The first part of the name is the genus and the second is the species. Most scientific names come from Latin or Greek. For example *Danaus plexippus* is the scientific name for the monarch butterfly. There are other related species of butterflies in the genus *Danaus* (each with a double name starting with *"Danaus"*), and in turn they are part of the butterfly family Nymphalidae, which in turn is in the order Lepidoptera, which consists of all butterflies and moths.

SEDIMENTARY ROCK: rocks that are formed by the gradual depositing of soil, sand, minerals, or other loose material over the surface of Earth or over the bottom of bodies of water. Sedimentary rocks are deposited in layers that can be dated.

TEMPERATE ZONE: that part of Earth's surface located between the tropics and the polar regions. The temperate zone is characterized by a warm summer and a cool winter.

TERRITORIAL: relating to animals that carefully guard an area considered to be their own. For example, a male giant helicopter damselfly guards a tree hole from other males, so that he is the one who gets the opportunity to mate with a female, who will then lay her eggs in the puddle of water inside the tree hole.

THORAX: the part of the body between the head and the abdomen. In insects, the wings and legs are attached to the thorax.

TOXICITY: the quality of being toxic or poisonous to an organism

TRANSPARENT: allowing light to pass through, as in see-through

TROPICAL ZONE: the part of Earth's surface surrounding the Equator. The tropics are characterized by a hot climate year round.

TRUE BUGS: any insect in the order Hemiptera, such as aphids, assassin bugs, cicadas, and giant water bugs. True bugs have piercing and sucking mouthparts.

VERTEBRATE: an organism with a backbone. Vertebrates can include mammals, fish, reptiles, amphibians, and birds.

MOVIES

BBC

Life: Insects: Episode 6 in season one of this acclaimed series about life on Earth focuses on insects, taking viewers right into the hives of honeybees and showing the journeys of monarch butterflies.

Life in the Undergrowth (2006): The camera focuses on the hidden lives of insects, unfolding in secret all around us.

Microcosmos (1996): This documentary includes amazing close-up footage of small-scale events, such as the growth of a mosquito, and ants at work.

Nature

Alien Empire (1995): This documentary explores insect body structure, migration, and means of survival.

Silence of the Bees (2008): The disappearance of bees resulting from the mysterious condition known as colony collapse disorder is examined in this film.

NOVA

Ants: Little Creatures Who Run the World: This documentary explores the lives of ant species around the world.

Bees: Tales From the Hive: Dive right into a hive and see what it's like to be a honeybee.

The Incredible Journey of the Butterflies: This film tells about the amazing yearly migration of monarch butterflies.

The Unknown World: The camera gets up close and personal with insects and other tiny creatures that live around us— and on us!

PLACES TO VISIT

U.S.A.:

Insect Zoo, Natural History Museum of Los Angeles County, California

University of Arkansas Arthropod Museum, Fayetteville, Arkansas

Insect Zoo, San Francisco Zoo, San Francisco, California

Bohart Museum of Entomology, Davis, California

The Butterfly Pavilion, Westminster, Colorado

Butterfly World, Coconut Creek, Florida

University of Georgia Insect Zoo, Athens, Georgia

K-State Insect Zoo, Manhattan, Kansas

Audubon Butterfly Garden and Insectarium, New Orleans, Louisiana

Butterfly House, Missouri Botanical Garden, Chesterfield, Missouri

Bayer Insectarium, St. Louis Zoo, St. Louis, Missouri

Magic Wings Butterfly House and Bayer CropScience Insectarium, Museum of Life and Science, Durham, North Carolina

World of the Insect, Cincinnati Zoo, Cincinnati, Ohio

Insect Zoo, Oregon Zoo, Portland, Oregon

Brown Hall of Entomology and Cockrell Butterfly Center, Houston Museum of Natural Science, Houston, Texas

Insectropolis, Toms River, New Jersey

O. Orkin Insect Zoo, Butterfly Pavilion, Smithsonian National Museum of Natural History, Washington, D.C.

Invertebrate Exhibit, National Zoo, Washington, D.C.

Outside U.S.A.:

Canada

Insectarium de Quebec, Montreal, Quebec

Victoria Butterfly Gardens, Brentwood Bay, British Columbia

Victoria Bug Zoo, Victoria, British Columbia

Lyman Entomological Museum and Research Laboratory, McGill University, Ste-Anne-de-Bellevue, Quebec

Niagara Parks Butterfly Conservatory, Niagara Falls, Ontario

Newfoundland Insectarium, Reidville, Newfoundland

South/Central America

Shipstern Nature Reserve, Belize (It has a butterfly garden.)

The Butterfly Farm, La Guacima de Alajuela, Costa Rica

Europe

London Zoo, London, England (It has an insect house called BUGS [Biodiversity Underpinning Global Survival].)

Artis Royal Zoo, Amsterdam, Netherlands (It has a butterfly pavilion and insectariums.)

Cologne Zoological Garden, Cologne, Germany (It has an insectarium.)

Budapest Zoo, Budapest, Hungary (It has insects and a butterfly pavilion.)

Wilhelma Zoological and Botanic Garden, Stuttgart, Germany (It has an insectarium.)

Bristol Zoo, Bristol, England (It has a bug world.)

Butterfly Park Benalmádena, Benalmádena, Malaga, Spain

Micropolis, Aveyron, France (It has an insect museum.)

Asia

Siam Insect-Zoo and Museum, Mae Rim, Thailand

Zoo Negara, Hulu Kelang, Selangor Darul Ehsan, Malaysia (It has an insect zoo with 200 species.)

Tama Zoo, Tokyo, Japan (It has an insectarium.)

Entopia, Penang, Malaysia

Insectarium, Hiroshima City Forest Park, Hiroshima, Japan

Bangkok Butterfly Garden and Insectarium, Bangkok, Thailand

Australia

Melbourne Museum, Melbourne (It has a Bugs Alive! permanent exhibit.)

Melbourne Zoo, Parkville, Victoria (It has a butterfly house and bug exhibit.)

INDEX

INDEX

PHOTO CREDITS

AD=Adobe Stock; AL=Alamy Stock Photo; GI=Getty Images; MP=Minden Pictures; NGIC=National Geographic Image Collection; NPL=Nature Picture Library; SS=Shutterstock

Front Cover: (grasshopper), David Brownell/AD; (pink moth), Kim Taylor/NPL; (shield bug), Sriyana/SS; (dung beetle), Cosmin Manci/SS; (red speckled beetle), Mark Brandon/SS; (damselfly), Henri Koskinen/SS; (tortoise beetle), Hendroh/SS; (blue morpho butterfly), Marc Bruxelle/SS; (caterpillar), BrightSpace/SS; (leaf), AmazeinDesign/SS; (wasp), Kletr/SS; (Cairns birdwing butterfly), johnbraid/SS; (ants), asharkyu/SS; (green beetle), Ale-ks/iStockphoto/GI; (ladybug), Ale-ks/iStockphoto/GI; **Back Cover:** Henk/AD; (background), Triff/SS; **Front Matter:** 1, ondreicka/AD; 2-3, mrobert67/SS; 4 (UP), irin-k/SS; 4 (CTR), Kesu/SS; 4 (LO LE), Eric Isselee/SS; 4 (LO RT), Cosmin Manci/SS; 4-5 (background), Triff/SS; 5 (UP LE), Cathy Keifer/SS; 5 (UP CTR), Hendroh/SS; 5 (UP RT), chinahbzyg/SS; 5 (LO LE), Norbert Wu/MP; 5 (LO RT), Cathy Keifer/SS; 6 (UP LE), Kesu/SS; 6 (UP RT), Dr. Bill Lamp; 6 (CTR), alslutsky/SS; 6 (LO), gosphotodesign/SS; 7 (UP LE), Darlyne A. Murawski; 7 (UP CTR), Darlyne A. Murawski; 7 (UP RT), Alik Mulikov/AD; 7 (CTR), Darlyne A. Murawski; 7 (LO LE), irin-k/SS; 7 (LO RT), Darlyne A. Murawski; **Chapter 1:** 10 (UP LE), ihorhvozdetskiy/AD; 10 (UP RT), Jason S/SS; 10 (LO LE), nataba/AD; 10 (LO CTR), Satoshi Adachi/AD; 10 (LO RT), driftwood/AD; 10-11, Thomas Marent/MP; 12, Michael_Ibanes/AD; 12-13, Mayumi.K.Photography/AD; 13, Matt Jeppson/SS; 14, asbtkb/AD; 14-15, Asha_Joshi/SS; 15 (LO LE), Anchasa/AD; 15 (LO RT), Wasu Watcharadachaphong/SS; 16 (UP), Alberto Gonzalez/AD; 16 (LO), Bjoern Wylezich/SS; 17 (UP), Paul Zahl/NGIC; 17 (LO), Jacob Benner-Tufts University/Reuters; 18 (UP), artcasta/SS; 18 (LO), Sourabh/AD; 19 (UP), Vilainecrevette/SS; 19 (LO), skynetphoto/SS; 21 (UP LE), rabbitti/AD; 21 (UP RT), Sherry Lemcke/AD; 21 (CTR LE), leekris/AD; 21 (CTR RT), AttaBoyLuther/E+/GI; 21 (LO LE), Dwight R. Kuhn; 21 (LO CTR), Dwight R. Kuhn; 21 (LO RT), All Canada Photos/AL; 22, Roman Teteruk/SS; 23 (UP LE), Deep Desert Photo/AD; 23 (UP RT), Darren5907/AL; 23 (LO), Takashi Shinkai/Nature Production/MP; 24 (LE), sutthipong/AD; 24 (RT), Mushy/AD; 24-25, George Grall/AL; 25 (LE), Alex Hyde/NPL; 25 (RT), hwongcc/SS; 26 (UP), Geza Farkas/AD; 26 (LO), Amir Ridhwan/SS; 27 (UP LE), Gerry/AD; 27 (UP RT), Melola/SS; 27 (LO), backiris/AD; 28 (UP), Digital Media Pro/SS; 28 (LO LE), jayvee18/AD; 28 (LO RT), Darlyne A. Murawski/NGIC; 29 (UP), Barry/AD; 29 (LO), Avalon.red/AL; 30 (LE), Cathy Keifer/AD; 30 (RT), mauritius images GmbH/AL; 30-31, Claudia Steininger/iStockphoto/GI; 31 (UP), Gypsy Picture Show/AD; 31 (CTR), Sarin Kunthong/SS; 31 (LO LE), John Abbott/NPL; 31 (LO RT), Andy Sands/NPL; 32-33 (LO), kozorog/AD; 33 (UP), Nature's Images/Science Source; 33 (LO), Aflo/NPL; 34, George Grall/NGIC; 35 (A), Eye of Science/Science Source; 35 (B), Vitalii Hulai/AD; 35 (C), Dwight R. Kuhn; 35 (D), Gerry Bishop/SS; 35 (E), Biehler Michael/SS; 35 (F), George Grall/NGIC; 35 (G), Ricardo/AD; 35 (H), dong-sushin/SS; 35 (I), darina1761/AD; 35 (J), Oleksii/AD; 35 (K), Dennis Kunkel Microscopy, Inc./Visuals Unlimited; 36 (CTR RT), Mircea Costina/Dreamstime; 36 (LE), Ch'ien Lee/MP; 36 (LO RT), stigmatize/SS; 37 (UP LE), moneycue_canada/AD; 37 (UP RT), Nigel Cattlin/Science Source; 37 (LO LE), Chris Alcock/SS; 37 (LO CTR), Tara L/SS; 37 (LO RT), Stephen Dalton/

MP; 38 (UP), Piotr Naskrecki/MP; 38 (LO), leekris/AD; 39 (UP), Greta/AD; 39 (CTR), BeeBatch/AD; 39 (LO), Piotr Naskrecki/MP; 40-41, vblinov/SS; 40 (LE), SergeyIT/SS; 40 (RT), Tan Hung Meng/SS; 41 (LE), Piotr Naskrecki/MP; 41 (CTR), Piotr Naskrecki/MP; 41 (RT), Piotr Naskrecki/MP; 42 (UP), Thomas Ames, Jr./Visuals Unlimited; 42 (LO), ilker canikligil/SS; 43 (UP), Masyanya/Dreamstime; 43 (CTR), Kenneth Bart/Visuals Unlimited; 43 (LO), Thorsten Schier/SS; 44 (UP), Satoshi Kuribayashi/Nature Production/MP; 44 (LO), Craig Taylor/SS; 45 (UP), B Norris/SS; 45 (LO LE), ondreicka/AD; 45 (LO RT), apassara/AD; 46 (LE), ondreicka/AD; 46 (RT), Darlyne A. Murawski/NGIC; 47 (UP LE), Adam Jones/Danita Delimont/AD; 47 (UP RT), Norbert Wu/MP; 47 (CTR LE), John Cancalosi/NPL; 47 (CTR RT), Young Swee Ming/SS; 47 (LO), Achisatha/AD; 48 (UP), Salaithip Chaimongkol/EyeEm/GI; 48 (LO), Yojik/SS; 49 (A), panyajampatong/AD; 49 (B), snvv18870020330/SS; 49 (C), blickwinkel/AL; 49 (D), kosssmosss/AD; 49 (E), Ch'ien Lee/MP; 49 (F), Alex Wild Photography; 49 (G), Wiratchai wansamngam/SS; 49 (H), S.Picavet/GI; 49 (I), hwongcc/SS; 49 (J), Dwight R. Kuhn; 49 (K), Maksimilian/SS; 50 (monarch butterfly), Sari ONeal/SS; 51 (diamondback moth), Olaf Leillinger; 51 (hoverfly), Ruckszio/AD; 51 (painted lady butterfly), Valery Kirsanov/SS; 51 (hummingbird hawk-moth), Studio Trebuchet/AD; 51 (armyworm moth), Donald Hobern; 51 (brown planthopper), Nigel Cattlin/FLPA/MP; 51 (dark blue tiger moth), J.M.Garg; 51 (desert locust), Eric Isselée/SS; 51 (globe skimmer dragonfly), Danita Delimont/SS; 51 (Madagascan sunset moth), ilker canikligil/SS; 51 (Bogong moth), Donald Hobern; 52, Matt Howard/SS; 52-53, 169169/AD; 53, Protasov AN/SS; 54, Stock Connection Blue/AL; 55 (A), Triff/SS; 55 (B), Stephane Bidouze/SS; 55 (C), Przemyslaw Wasilewski/SS; 55 (D), akiyoko/SS; 55 (E), WvdM/SS; 55 (F), Thor Jorgen Udvang/SS; 55 (G), Pavel L Photo and Video/SS; 55 (H), TSpider/SS; 55 (I), mycola/SS; 55 (J), Peter Gudella/SS; 55 (K), Carolina K. Smith MD/SS; **Chapter 2:** 56-57, Stefan Holm/500px Plus/GI; 57 (UP LE), Piotr Naskrecki/MP; 57 (UP CTR), chinahbzyg/SS; 57 (UP RT), Ingo Arndt/MP; 57 (LO LE), Darlyne A. Murawski/NGIC; 57 (LO RT), Michael Durham/MP; 58 (UP), Nigel Cattlin/AL; 58 (CTR), blickwinkel/AL; 58 (LO), Graham Montgomery; 58-59, Cyril Ruoso/NPL; 60, Chris Mattison/NPL; 61, Iliuta/AD; 62, Jan Hamrsky/NPL; 63, Bob Jensen/Photoshot; 64, Hanne & Jens Eriksen/NPL; 65, Danita Delimont/SS; 66 (UP), Earnest Tse/AD; 66 (LO LE), Petr Ganaj/SS; 66 (LO RT), Abeselom Zerit/AD; 67 (UP), Tomas1111/SS; 67 (LO LE), finchfocus/SS; 67 (LO RT), Rod Gardner/AD; 68, Mark Moffett/MP; 69, Steve Collins; 70, Susan & Allan Parker/AL; 71, Floriana/AD; 72, Eric Isselée/AD; 73, Dmitry Zhukov/AD; 74, Piotr Naskrecki/MP; 75, Piotr Naskrecki/MP; 76, Jumping-Spiderss/SS; 77, Bartomeu Borrell/Collection/Photoshot; 78, Pluto Mc/AD; 79, Sonja Wedmann; 80, Yi fang/Imaginechina/Associated Press; 81, Yi fang/Imaginechina/Associated Press; 82, traitsun/SS; 83, Picture-Alliance/dpa/age fotostock; 84, UlkaAStudio/SS; 85, Geraldas/AD; 86, James H RobinsonPhoto Researchers RM/GI; 87, SailingAway/AD; 88, Dietmar Nill/Foto Natura/MP; 89, F1online digitale Bildagentur GmbH/AL; 90 (LE), Stephen Dalton/SS; 90 (RT), v_blinov/AD; 90-91, Nadine/AD; 91 (UP), Doug Lemke/SS; 91 (LO LE), George Grall/AL; 91 (LO RT), chris2766/AD; 92, Biosphoto/AL; 93, Mitsuhiko Imamori/MP; 94, Muellek Josef/SS; 95, Kristina Postnikova/SS; 96 (LE), abdul gapur dayak/AD; 96 (RT), Sergei Detyukov/AD;

96-97, Sebastian/AD ; 97 (UP), Edwin Giesbers/NPL; 97 (LO LE), Ehrman Photographic/SS; 97 (LO RT), Roger Meerts/SS; 98, fritz16/SS; 99, Peter Essick/NGIC; 99 (inset), Peter Essick/NGIC; 100, Andrew Newman Nature Pictures/AL; 101, Kim Taylor/NPL; 102, Darlyne A. Murawski/NGIC; 103, Garna Zarina/SS; 104, Frans Lanting/Mint Images/GI; 105, Phil Savoie/NPL; 106, Densey Clyne/AUSCAPE; 107, Skip Moody/Dembinsky Photo Associates/AL; 108, Darlyne A. Murawski/NGIC; 109, George Grall/NGIC; 110 (LE), William Fehr/AD; 110 (RT), Darlyne A. Murawski/NGIC; 110-111, Valeriy Kirsanov/AD; 111 (UP), Valeriy Kirsanov/AD; 111 (LO LE), Gerry/AD; 111 (LO RT), Lori Epstein/age fotostock; 112, Ingo Arndt/MP; 112 (inset), Darlyne A. Murawski/NGIC; 113, Karl Gehring/The Denver Post/GI; 114, Kazuo Unno/Nature Production/MP; 115, Mitsuhiko Imamori/MP; 116, Paul Zahl/NGIC; 117, Mitsuhiko Imamori/MP; 118, Martin Shields/AL; 119, George Grall/NGIC; 120 (LE), Javier Aznar Gonzalez de Rueda/NGIC; 120 (RT), Vinicius R. Souza/SS; 120-121, Javier Aznar Gonzalez de Rueda/NGIC; 121 (UP), Marcus Kam/SS; 121 (LO LE), Paul Zahl/NGIC; 121 (LO RT), George Grall/NGIC; 122, Victor/AD; 123, Darlyne A. Murawski/NGIC; 124, KHBlack/AD; 125, Greg Brave/iStockphoto/GI; 126 (LE), Sweeming Young/AD; 126 (RT), Joshua Daniels/AD; 126-127, Sandeep/AD; 127 (UP), nawin/AD; 127 (LO LE), skynet/AD; 127 (LO RT), cbstockfoto/AL; 128, David Liittschwager/NGIC; 129, JGade/AD; 130, Husni Che Ngah/Biosphoto/MP; 131, Flickr RF/GI; 132, John Cancalosi/AL; 133, Joel Sartore/NGIC; 134, Jan Miko/SS; 135, Bianca Lavies/NGIC; 136, Oleg Golovnev/SS; 137, Clarence Holmes Wildlife/AL; 138, Dwight R. Kuhn; 139, Petr/AD; 140-141, chinahbzyg/SS; 141, pixelman/SS; **Chapter 3:** 142-143, Dmytro Surkov/AD; 142 (UP LE), Eric Isselee/SS; 142 (UP CTR), smuay/SS; 142 (UP RT), Peeravit/SS; 142 (LO LE), leekris/AD; 142 (LO RT), kurt_G/SS; 144-145, nicholashan/AD; 146, Protasov AN/SS; 147, mehmetkrc/AD; 147 (inset), KKphotographer/SS; 148, Tompel/SS; 149, Henrik Larsson/SS; 150 (LE), muhammad hasan faiz/SS; 150 (RT), kurt_G/SS; 150-151, Mark Moffett/MP; 151 (UP), Dr. Morley Read/SS; 151 (LO LE), David Liittschwager/NGIC; 151 (LO RT), Paul Zahl/NGIC; 152, Ch'ien Lee/MP; 153, Ch'ien Lee/MP; 154, Satoshi Kuribayashi/Nature Production/MP; 155, Stephen Dalton/NPL; 156, Yonhap, Choi Byung-kil/Associated Press; 157, khlungcenter/SS; 157 (inset), Lori Epstein/age fotostock; 158 (LF), M. Maruyama; 158 (RT), D. Kronauer; 159, M. Maruyama; 160, Piotr Naskrecki/MP; 161, Petr Muckstein/SS; 162, Kenneth Garrett/NGIC; 163, Joel Sartore/NGIC; 164, Nigel Cattlin/NPL; 165, Robert Harding World Imagery/GI; 166, David Liittschwager/NGIC; 167, Paul Zahl/NGIC; 168, Paul Reeves/SS; 169, Crystal Ernst/170, Joel Sartore/NGIC; 171, John T. Fowler/AL; 172, Paul Bertner/AD; 173, David Liittschwager/NGIC; 174, Michael & Patricia Fogden/MP; 175, Muuhy/AD; 176, Thomas Marent/MP; 177, Satoshi Kuribayashi/Nature Production/MP; 178 (LE), Pan Xunbin/SS; 178 (RT), kurt_G/SS; 178-179, Kamila Sankiewicz/AD; 179 (UP), Darlyne A. Murawski/NGIC; 179 (LO LE), Kevin/AD; 179 (LO RT), constantincornel/AD; 180, Alex Hyde/NPL; 181, Vinicius R. Souza/SS; 182 (LE), Frank Hecker; 182 (RT), errni/SS; 183, Armen/AD; 184, constantincornel/AD; 185, Nigel Cattlin/FLPA/MP; 186, Gaëlle Doitteau/Muséum national d'Histoire naturelle, Paris (France), Collection: Paleontology (F), Fossil specimen MNHN.F.R10411; 187, imageBROKER/drL. Werle/age fotostock; 188, Evelyn/AD; 189, Tonia Graves/AL; 190, Sandy Millar/Wirestock/AD; 191, JJ Gouin/2; 192, Rob Carr/Associated Press; 193, Bernard Lynch/Moment RF/GI; 194, Aynia Brennan/SS; 195, Anton Sorokin/AL; 196, Victorian Traditions/SS; 197, Richard Becker/FLPA/MP; 197 (inset), PHOTO FUN/SS; 198, George Grall/NGIC; 200 (LE), Kim Taylor/NPL; 200 (RT), milkovasa/AD;

200-201, A.N.T. Photo Library/NHPA/Photoshot; 201 (UP), Mircea Costina/SS; 201 (LO LE), Claire Haskins/AD; 201 (LO RT), Jennifer Read and Dr. John Huber/Canadian National Collection of Insects, Arachnids and Nematodes; 202, Tacio Philip/AD; 203, BeeApiaries/AD; 203 (inset), willypd/AD; 204, Erhard Nerger/imageBROKER/AL; 205, MarkMirror/SS; 206, Possent phsycography/SS; 207, yod67/AD; 208, Robert Sisson/NGIC; 209, Alex Wild/Visuals Unlimited/GI; 210 (LE), Mark Moffett/NGIC; 210 (RT), Midnight Studio TH/SS; 211, Mark Moffett/MP; 212, Peter Finch/Stone RF/GI; 212 (inset), Peter Essick/NGIC; 213, Mark W. Moffett/NGIC; 214, CStock/AD; 215, Vovantarakan/SS; 216, Stephen Dalton/MP; 217, Darlyne A. Murawski/NGIC; 218, Piotr Naskrecki/MP; 219, Alex Wild Photography; 220, Alex Wild Photography; 221, blickwinkel/AL; 222, Jeffrey Van Daele/Dreamstime; 222 (inset), János Kerekes Photography/Moment RF/GI; 223, Saidin Jusoh/AD; 224, David Liittschwager/NGIC; 225, Rolf Müller/AD; 226, Paul Zahl/NGIC; 227, Solvin Zankl/NPL; 228, Nigel Cattlin/NPL; 229, Jean Lecomte/Biosphoto; 230, Sinclair Stammers/Science Source; 231, David Liittschwager/NGIC; 232, Classic/AD; 233, Vinicius R. Souza/SS; 234, Dr. Alice Wells; 235, Picavet/Workbook Stock/GI; 236, Tadeas Skuhra/SS; 237, Dobermaraner/SS; 238 (inset), Cathy Keifer/SS; 238 (inset), Jason Patrick Ross/SS; 239, Mike Gustafson/AD; 240, Ed Reschke/Photodisc/GI; 241, Jak Wonderly/NGP; 242, Florian Andronache/SS; 243, Darlyne A. Murawski/NGIC; 244, Robert Clark/NGIC; 245, Nirut Sangkeaw/AD; 246, Darrell Gulin/Danita Delimont/AD; 247, Darlyne A. Murawski/NGIC; 248, Maksimilian/SS; 249, Belozorova Elena/SS; 250, Dmitrii/AD; 251, Joel Sartore/NGIC; 252 (LE), johnbraid/SS; 252 (RT), Sander Meertins/AD; 252-253, jonnysek/AD; 253 (UP), KCEmperor/SS; 253 (LO LE), Nikola Rahme/SS; 253 (LO RT), M. Williams Woodbridge/NGIC; 254, bimserd/AD; 255, Cocos.Bounty/SS; 256, Jussi Lindberg/SS; 257, Ingo Arndt/Foto Natura/MP; 258, Auscape International Pty Ltd/AL; 259, Jiri Lochman/NPL; 260, Nick Garbutt/NPL; 261, The Natural History Museum/AL; 262, Roy Toft/NGIC; 264, akhug/AD; 265, Melinda Tawver/SS; 265 (inset), Edward Brubaker/iStockphoto/AD; 266, Dr. Hans Banziger; 267, Dr. Hans Banziger; 268 (LE), Darlyne A. Murawski/NGIC; 268 (RT), George Grall/NGIC; 268-269, George Grall/NGIC; 269 (UP), David Halgrimson/AD; 269 (LO LE), George Grall/NGIC; 269 (LO RT), George Grall/NGIC; **Chapter 4:** 270-271, lukjonis/AD; 271 (UP LE), ondreicka/AD; 271 (UP CTR), Cathy Keifer/SS; 271 (UP RT), Helene Schmitz/NGIC; 271 (LO LE), Diarmuid/AD; 271 (LO RT), Darlyne A. Murawski/NGIC; 272-273, SDeming/SS; 273, Jonathan Lewis/Oxford Scientific RM/GI; 274 (UP LE), ysk/AD; 274 (LO LE), Satoshi Kuribayashi/Nature Production/MP; 274 (LO RT), Yudha Pratama/SS; 274-275, Radka Palenikova/SS; 275 (UP), Stephen Dalton/MP; 275 (LO LE), Gerry Ellis/Digital Vision; 275 (LO RT), Ingram Dirra; 276 (UP), Emanuele Biggi/NPL; 276 (LO LE), Paul Rollins/AL; 276 (LO RT), Ilga/AD; 277 (UP), peter/AD, 277 (LO LE), Hans Christoph Kappel/NPL; 277 (LO RT), Greg Forcey/AL; **Chapter 5:** 278-279, jps/SS; 278 (UP LE), Vladimir Kim/SS; 278 (UP CTR), Reality-Images/SS; 278 (UP RT), Mirvav/SS; 278 (LO LE), Lukas Jonaitis/SS; 278 (LO RT), Doug Lemke/SS; 280 (UP), courtesy Bill Lamp; 280 (LO), John Davidson; 281, lawcain/AD; 282 (UP), SS; 282 (LO), Dave Bevan/AL; 283 (LE), Alik Mulikov/SS; 283 (RT), Grtechen Stuppy Carlson; 284 (LE), Aflo/NPL; 284 (RT), Pan Xunbin/SS; 285 (UP), Jacob Benner-Tufts Unversity/Reuters; 285 (LO), Vilainecrevette/SS; 286, chinahbzyg/SS; 287, Mitsuhiko Imamori/MP; 288 (LE), Alik Mulikov/AD; 288 (RT), irin-k/SS; 296, khlungcenter/SS; **Page 296:** (UP), Darlyne A. Murawski; (CTR), Nancy Honovich; (LO), Dr. Bill Lamp

Published by Collins
An imprint of HarperCollins Publishers
1 Robroyston Gate, Glasgow G33 1JN
www.harpercollins.co.uk

HarperCollins Publishers
Macken House, 39/40 Mayor Street Upper, Dublin 1
D01 C9W8
Ireland

© 2024 National Geographic Partners LLC. All rights reserved.
NATIONAL GEOGRAPHIC KIDS and Yellow Border Design are
trademarks of National Geographic Society, used under license.

First published 2024
This edition 2026

ISBN 9780008825188

10 9 8 7 6 5 4 3 2 1

Designed by Sanjida Rashid
Photo direction by Lori Epstein

This edition of Ultimate Bugopedia was updated and expanded
by Darlyne Murawski.

The publisher acknowledges and thanks Darlyne Murawski and
Bill Lamp for their expert insight and guidance. Many thanks
also to project manager Priyanka Lamichhane and researcher
Michelle Harris for their invaluable assistance with this book.

Darlyne MURAWSKI

Author Darlyne Murawski is a nature photographer and former research biologist with degrees in biology and art. Much of her work focuses on small and sometimes overlooked topics such as moths, spiders, parasites, diatoms, worms, reptiles, and fungi, which she frequently showcases in school presentations. Her previous books include *Face to Face With Caterpillars*, *Bug Faces*, and *Spiders and Their Webs*. Her work has appeared in many publications, including *National Geographic* magazine and children's magazines.

Nancy HONOVICH

Nancy Honovich is a New York City–based writer and editor who specializes in books for children and young adults. Her favorite insect is the mole cricket.

Bill LAMP

Expert consultant Bill Lamp, a Nebraska native and University of Maryland professor, became an entomologist the day he discovered aquatic insects in the headwaters of the Mississippi River. Though he has been bitten by hellgrammites, stabbed by tabanid larvae, and stung by vespid wasps, the amazing and intricate behaviors of insects keep Bill exploring new habitats and species. With more than 90 publications on aquatic and pest insect ecology, Bill enjoys sharing his enthusiasm for entomology with his wonderful students, wife, children, and grandchildren.